Raising the bar

How household incomes can grow the way they used to

Edited by Andrew Harrop

About the authors

Torsten Bell is director of the Resolution Foundation.

Dustin Benton is policy director at Green Alliance.

Craig Berry is reader in political economy at the Future Economies Research Centre, Manchester Metropolitan University.

Anneliese Dodds is Labour MP for Oxford East and a shadow Treasury minister.

Alexander Guschanski is a researcher at the Greenwich Political Economy Research Centre, University of Greenwich.

Andrew Harrop is general secretary of the Fabian Society.

John Mills is founder and chairman of JML and an economic commentator.

Özlem Onaran is professor of economics at the University of Greenwich and the director of the Greenwich Political Economy Research Centre.

Chi Onwurah is Labour MP for Newcastle upon Tyne Central and shadow minister for industrial strategy, science and innovation.

Rachel Reeves is Labour MP for Leeds West and chair of the business, energy and industrial strategy select committee.

Geoff Tily is senior economist at the TUC.

CONTENTS

INTRODUCTION

Andrew Harrop

Four years ago, a Fabian report argued that GDP should no longer be the main measure of national economic success. Instead we should judge our economy by the pace at which ordinary household incomes rise; after all, the point of economic growth is to place prosperity into the hands of the people.

Judged by this benchmark, the UK's recent economic record is truly terrible. Before the financial crisis, median household incomes used to grow on average by more than 2 per cent a year. This was not a short-term phenomenon linked to a fragile pre-crisis economy. It was the long-term British trend, seen ever since the Second World War. By contrast, after the financial crisis, family incomes have barely grown at all. The real incomes of working-age households are only just higher than those of 2007.

So how can we get family incomes to grow the way they used to? That is the simple question the Fabian Society posed to the authors of this pamphlet. We wanted to understand what it might take to get back to the 'old normal' – the regular rising income that half a generation of workers have never seen. In doing this, our aim has been to take on the sense of fatalism that has overtaken Britain's economic debate, to prove that the UK does not have to settle for the growth we have.

1

Right now it feels like the pillars of the economic establishment are planning for stagnation. The Bank of England and the Office for Budget Responsibility base their forecasts on the assumption that real wages will barely rise. Their most recent projections imply that median earnings will not reach their 2007 levels until well into the 2020s. And we're now in the extraordinary position where the economy is believed to be 'over-heating', to the extent that interest rate rises are required, even though household incomes are barely rising.

And because of these projections, the Conservatives have not finished with austerity. They are still planning big cuts to social security, which will further reduce the incomes of the bottom half and hugely increase child poverty over the next five years. It is important to remember that, while earnings are the most important component of family incomes, if wages are rising while benefits are falling, living standards will be held back.

Cuts to benefits and tax credits have a direct impact on household incomes. But cuts in public services and investment have also had a terrible impact on households, by suppressing growth in GDP and earnings. In his chapter Geoff Tily makes a compelling case for ending austerity and raising public spending for the sake of growth. He shows that stimulating demand through public spending will lead to higher hourly earnings and productivity. And since this will lead economists to re-assess whether the economy is at full capacity, Tily argues that interest rates should not be raised until there is evidence of domestically-induced inflation.

There are other macro-economic proposals in the report too. Özlem Onaran and Alexander Gushanski demonstrate that less inequality will lead to higher, more stable growth. Action on inequality is a win/win for family incomes, because it grows the size of the economic pie and the share of t that low and middle-income households receive. They offer a comprehensive list of actions to narrow the income gap.

Meanwhile John Mills argues that the economy will not be able to grow fast again until the UK has a larger manufacturing sector and can reduce its huge trade deficit. He proposes a managed exchange rate to deliver a permanent and credible devaluation that will give businesses the certainty to invest. The possible long-term benefits of devaluation need to be balanced against the short-term disadvantage of inflation, however. In his contribution Torsten Bell explains how economic shocks that caused inflation have been rapidly transmitted into lower real wages because we have a flexible labour market where workers are in a weak position to insist on higher pay.

Bell is joined by Tily, Onaran and Gushanski, and by Rachel Reeves in arguing that a less flexible labour market is a strategy for income growth. Intervention to make modern work less precarious and to boost workplace collectivism is needed to redress power imbalances and enable workers to bargain for decent pay rises. This must be a priority for the left, not just for the sake of fairness but for our national prosperity.

Bell also argues for continued action in areas of recent progress, namely tackling low pay and achieving full employment. The national living wage should be gradually extended to younger age-groups and more action is needed to secure high employment for mothers (who could be put off from working by universal credit), disabled people and those in low-employment economies like Birmingham.

More generally, sensitivity to place is essential if household incomes are to start growing again. Craig Berry sets out a comprehensive agenda for reducing regional inequalities, with calls for the fair geographic distribution of public investment, beefed-up powers of local and regional economic leadership, keeping public money within local economies, and supporting stronger manufacturing supply chains.

Rachel Reeves and Chi Onwurah also emphasise the need for regionally balanced growth in discussing industrial strategy. Reeves examines the 'everyday economy', the high-volume, low-paid jobs found everywhere. She calls for a national strategy for good work, linked to new sector deals for service sectors like retail and social care.

Onwurah's focus is on the economic sectors of the future. She argues for mission-oriented innovation where the public sector shapes and steers the economy's development, through strategic investment and leadership. One mission she identifies is to push towards a big rise in research and development spending and the percentage of high-skill jobs. Her other mission is to embrace green technologies and clean energy and this is the focus of Dustin Benton's contribution. He argues that not only is green growth essential to meet our environmental obligations, it is also good for household incomes because it raises business productivity, opens new export markets and creates valuable mid-skill jobs.

From cracking down down on zero-hours contracts to investing in the green economy, this is a wide-ranging agenda for raising earnings. These and many of the other proposals are both the right actions to pursue in themselves and good for living standards. But while it is correct to focus on the primacy of boosting wages, we must not forget that the welfare state also has a vital role to play. The social infrastructure of strong public services and the income top-ups of redistributive social security are essential for family prosperity too.

In order to end austerity and reinvest in the welfare state, however, taxes will probably need to rise. These increases must be levied on those with the broadest shoulders, to ensure they do not put a dent in ordinary post-tax incomes.

4

So in her chapter Anneliese Dodds makes the case for rebalancing the tax system so that rich individuals and large companies pay more. It is the final component in this progressive agenda for getting household incomes to grow, just the way they used to.

A Fabian Society agenda for raising household incomes

Across the different chapters our contributors propose these measures for raising household incomes:

Fiscal and monetary policy: end austerity by stopping public spending from falling as a percentage of GDP; increase public investment; only raise interest rates when there is evidence of domestically driven inflation; consider a managed exchange rate as part of monetary policy.

Labour market reform: introduce a national 'good jobs' strategy, as part of sector deals with low-paying industries; increase the regulation of zero-hours and variable-hours jobs; end tax incentives for employers which incentivise self-employment and very short hours; increase and broaden the national living wage unless there is clear evidence of negative employment impacts; re-design universal credit to make work pay for mothers; increase support for disabled workers to retain jobs.

Worker collectivism: increase powers for trade unions including unimpeded access to workplaces and electronic balloting; introduce workers on boards and sector-level partnerships between employers and unions; government support for new forms of collective organisation, especially for the self-employed, and for alternative models of business ownership which give workers more control and reward.

Regional policy: devolve strong economic powers to local and regional authorities; distribute public investment fairly across the country; encourage public bodies and other local 'anchor' institutions to spend their money locally and include employment conditions in procurement contracts; create a 10 Downing Street 'local wealth unit' to drive stronger local leadership capacity.

Industrial strategy: design industrial strategy around national missions; support manufacturing supply chain development; seek to significantly increase public and private R&D spending; maintain strong environmental regulation and targets to promote world-leading green technologies; develop sectoral strategies for 'everyday' jobs; establish a network of regional investment banks.

Redistribution: rebalance the tax system to raise more from rich individuals and large corporations; review all tax reliefs and allowances; end social security cuts.

1: A NATIONAL MISSION: INDUSTRIAL STRATEGY FOR THE ECONOMY WE WANT

Chi Onwurah

To grow household incomes sustainably we need an industrial strategy focused on delivering the future economy we want. In place of a financialised model which discourages productive investment, Britain requires a 'mission-orientated industrial strategy' where government directs investment towards the growth opportunities of the future.

In June last year, Labour might not have won the general election – but our message won hearts and minds across the country. We were able to inspire people of all ages and almost all backgrounds with a manifesto that offered hope. Off the back of this it's estimated that we won a majority of the votes cast by under-45s, and matched the Conservative vote share among 45 to 54-year-olds.

Our message was a positive one, but it was aided by a real sense that under the Conservatives the economy has been moving backwards for ordinary people. The austerity agenda – what I call George Osborne's zombie economics – has led to a crisis of social mobility and reduced the opportunities available to ordinary people. In the north-east we have felt this acutely: savage welfare cuts have led to 40,000 people depending on Trussell Trust food banks each year while we have seen 40 per cent of our SureStart centres close permanently.

Raising the bar

As a child growing up in Newcastle I benefited from a great comprehensive school, an affordable council house and a fantastic health service. That is how a poor, black, working-class girl could become a chartered engineer and, later, member of parliament for my home town. After eight years of Conservative rule I worry that the same opportunities are not available to my constituents now – the impact of austerity on public services is holding them back.

But what is also holding them back is Conservative failure on the economy, with family incomes stagnant since the financial crisis. According to the ONS, the value of median income for non-retired households was £29,300 in 2017, only £100 per year higher than in 2008.

The reality is that while the public sector has shrunk, our economy has failed to provide the jobs and wage growth people need. Today 3.8 million workers are in poverty across the UK – that's one in every eight – and 5.7 million are in jobs that pay less than the (true) living wage. Real wages have fallen 10 per cent in the last years, a drop comparable only to Greece among the developed countries. In the north-east, the average worker is £4,000 per year poorer than 10 years ago.

Longer term causes

Osbornomics, which continues in a different guise under his successor Philip Hammond, has been deeply damaging to our economy and to family incomes but it is nothing new. Since Margaret Thatcher, successive Conservative governments have been obsessed with cutting, deregulating and reducing the size of the state.

I'm proud of what Labour did when in power to reverse and cushion these trends, and indeed it was in the 2000s under a Labour government that we last saw a period of rapid and sustained growth in median household incomes. But we failed to fundamentally change our country's economic model and fully reverse the rollback of our public services.

We were told that with the state out of the way, the private sector would flourish. But what flourished instead is what academics and commentators call a 'financialised' economy – one dominated by market-based trading that creates profits without producing anything. Since Thatcher's 'big bang' in 1986, the growth of finance has outstripped all other UK sectors, and as a percentage of GDP our financial sector is now larger than that of any other G7 economy.

Financialisation

Financialisation has been a big success for shareholders and executives. But it has severely hampered our ability to produce wealth collectively and prevented the rewards of growth from being shared equally.

Investment in real stuff is risky. It involves putting money into costly productive capabilities that won't necessarily be fully utilised. Individuals, businesses, households and workers do this all the time. But the rules of our ultra-financialised economy dictate that the only economic actors who should be rewarded for the risks that they take are shareholders. Companies should therefore 'maximise shareholder value' at all costs.

And as world-leading economist Mariana Mazzucato argues in her new book The Value of Everything, this focus on maximising shareholder value has two consequences – what she calls the 'two faces of financialisation'. The first is that the financial sector stops resourcing the risky business of investing in 'real stuff'. Instead it favours behaviours – for instance share buybacks and financial engineering – that line the pockets of shareholders but don't necessarily add to the productive capacity of the economy. Rather than investing in companies which produce 'stuff', finance is financing finance. The second is the financialisation of the real economy, with industry driven by short-term returns when it is financed at all. This results in less reinvestment of profits and a rising burden of debt which, in a vicious cycle, makes industry even more driven by short-term considerations.

This kind of finance is not neutral but changes the nature of what it finances. It disincentivises the difficult, costly business of maintaining sunk assets like factories or developing new technologies, instead encouraging strategies – such as offshoring jobs – that neglect people and place but provide an immediate financial return. This is partially reflected in our country's low spending on research and development. Since the 1980s we have consistently been at or near the bottom of the league table of public and private R&D spend across developed countries. And in moving away from a manufacturing-led economy, we've sacrificed a reliable source of long-run wage growth.

The solution – mission-oriented innovation

To fix our economy's long-standing weaknesses and get family incomes growing like they used to, the government must do more than stimulate the economy and redistribute wealth. We need to ensure that we have broad-based economic growth in the first place – and we can do that with an industrial strategy based on a vision for the high-wage, high-skill, high-productivity economy that we want to build.

The last 40 years have shown us that it matters where growth comes from, as the absence of vibrant local economies destroys the fabric of communities, and damages quality of life. And, while the British economy needs to create value, it must create much more than just financial value in the form of shareholder profit – there must also be social value through the creation of jobs, goods and services so that we can all live richer lives in a richer Britain.

Mazzucato and Carlota Perez make a similar argument when they say: "It is important to emphasise the distinction between the potential of a technological revolution and the direction of investment and innovation in which that potential is deployed... the direction chosen for using the new potential across the economy becomes a socio-political choice."

But what does setting a 'direction' mean in practice? Mazzucato advocates what she calls a 'mission-oriented industrial strategy'. This means the public sector making strategic investments, not to take the place of the private sector but to encourage further investment from business and to catalyse innovation.

Investment is driven by business perceptions of where the future opportunities are for growth, and mission-oriented policies create these opportunities, bringing public and private sector investors together in pursuit of a shared goal. In its report on the Industrial Strategy Green Paper, the House of Commons Business, Energy and Industrial Strategy Select Committee endorsed this approach, recommending: "A 'mission-based' approach, shaped by a vision as to the direction we want the economy to move towards, underpinned by a foundation of strong horizontal policies." These recommendations were echoed by the non-partisan Industrial Strategy Commission based at Manchester and Sheffield Universities, and mission-oriented policies are also being explored by the European Commission.

Labour's plans

Labour's industrial strategy is founded on these principles. We recognise that our country has great strengths we can build on: our world-class universities and extraordinary heritage of scientific research, our booming creative industries; and our cutting-edge manufacturers, from ceramics to steel and to automotive. A Labour government will take bold steps to make the most of these strengths and provide support and investment where it is needed.

This is a more strategic and coordinated approach than we have seen in recent decades but it is not old-fashioned centralisation or command-and-control. It is about the state bringing workers and employers together with other stakeholders, and working with them in a way that is proactive, integrated, and long-term, drawing on best practices from other countries to preserve our existing strengths and create future winners.

Our approach is positive and practical. It speaks to the student anxious about his or her future, the single mum working two minimum wage jobs, and the Redcar steelworker wanting a job to be proud of. It addresses the crisis in productivity, skills and wages which keeps us poor even with unemployment relatively low.

We have set out two initial missions. First, to decarbonise the economy with 60 per cent of our energy drawn from renewable sources by 2030. Second, to build an 'innovation nation' with 3 per cent of our GDP spent on research and development and the highest percentage of highly skilled jobs in the OECD.

Achieving these missions will involve investment in skills, infrastructure and good, productive work. In government, Labour will take advantage of historically low interest rates to borrow £250bn for infrastructure spending over 10 years. We will set up a network of regional investment banks across the country. And we will create a National Education Service, allowing people to retrain throughout their lives. These are the foundations upon which we will get the economy growing and ensure family incomes start to rise again.

2: CATCHING UP: CLOSING THE REGIONAL INCOME DIVIDE

Craig Berry

Household incomes are lower in Britain's poorer regions and the gap has widened in recent decades. But attempts to address regional inequalities since the financial crash still rely on pre-crisis thinking. We need to go much further – managing the economy strategically, devolving real power to the regions and spending fairly on infrastructure – to bring growth to every part of Britain.

The north-south divide, albeit loosely defined, has long been part of the British pathos. The country's political elite has, ostensibly, often sought to address the very real geographical inequalities which underpin this rather simplistic trope. But the 2008 financial crisis led to an identifiable gear-shift, as the divide began to feature heavily in both elite and popular diagnoses of the crisis, and how Britain's subsequent economic malaise might be addressed.

Just because there is a will, however, it does not mean there is (yet) a way. The notion of 'rebalancing' has framed elite discourse since the crisis, in recognition of the economy's over-dependence on growth in London and the south-east. But in suggesting that Britain's economic model is fundamentally sound, but merely distended in some ways, rebalancing has not given rise to a suitably transformative policy agenda.

Related discourses such as the northern powerhouse and midlands engine are, at best, rather hollow – comically, on 18 August 2016, Theresa May published near-identical op-eds in The Yorkshire Post and The Birmingham Mail endorsing both agendas – and, at worst, quite infantilising. They put the emphasis on poorer regions needing to take responsibility for their own disadvantage, rather than the very longstanding political and economic inequalities that characterise our economy and structure the relationship between regions. They also overlook the roles that poorer regions play in supporting prosperity elsewhere in the economy.

Lower household incomes in poorer regions are one of the main signifiers of Britain's geographical inequalities. This inequality has worsened in recent decades, before and after the crisis, as a result of various downward pressures on earnings. Manufacturing industries once sustained earnings around the median point, but deindustrialisation – a process arguably dating back to the nineteenth century, but which accelerated from the 1980s – has hollowed out labour markets, particularly in the northern regions, the West Midlands and Wales.

The rise of low-value service industries has failed to fill the earnings gap. These industries are more dependent on local consumption, rather than exports, and are therefore held back by sluggish local earnings growth, a self-reinforcing trend which creates a low-wage equilibrium in many local economies. Wages in services industries have been driven further down by digitalisation, precarious employment practices and the consolidation of market share by key firms.

London and the south-east have not been immune from these trends. Just as we do not often enough consider the geographical dimension of the earnings squeeze, we also too quickly gloss over the fact that geographical differences in many ways reflect class-based inequalities. These inequalities are clearly evident in London and its hinterland – but as a whole these areas are more economically diverse.

Key industries in London and the south-east are also deemed more strategically significant within the national growth model, and therefore receive extensive public sector support. The growth of public sector employment in the north supported incomes in the 1990s and 2000s, but a reversal of this trend since 2010 has barely registered in London and the south-east.

The international context is crucial here too. As financial markets synchronise and production networks internationalise, the global capitalist system has changed in character, with new core/periphery dynamics rendering the divide between developed and developing worlds highly anachronistic. The globalist capitalist core consists instead of a network of large city-regions across the world.

London is Britain's only truly global city, due primarily to the finance sector's international significance, and how this shapes the capital's economy more generally. But whereas policy elites tend to present this apparent success story in isolation from the rest of the domestic economy, in reality London's global city status is buttressed by the import of human and financial resources from provincial regions, part of a dynamic some observers now refer to as a 'finance curse'.

Crucially, however, this process does not simply leave Britain's local economies starved of resources. It also offers significant power to London-centred firms, and their international partners, to reorder local economies for their own benefit. The way that outsourcing firms design contracts to extract value from local authorities, while leading the deterioration of local labour market conditions, offers an instructive example.

In this context, Brexit is the last thing Britain's disadvantaged regions need. One of the paradoxes of 'globalisation' is that trade has become more local: it is hard to trade services across long distances, and goods trade increasingly consists of components, via integrated production chains, rather than finished products.

The 'remainer' left will get nowhere pretending that EU membership has not buttressed London's privileged status, due to the City's entrepôt function for the Eurozone. Britain could not have remained outside the Eurozone indefinitely in these circumstances, and the European Commission's moves towards establishing authority over certain City functions is a key factor behind elite support for Brexit.

At the same time, however, single market and customs union membership is vital for maintaining what is left of Britain's manufacturing capacity, since production processes are highly integrated across the continent. Yet the perennial weakness of British industrial policy means this capacity has become concentrated in relatively isolated pockets of high-value manufacturing activity, often dependent on overseas firms, with limited integration with the local economies in which they are physically located.

This dynamic lies behind the 'left behind' phenomenon in smaller urban and coastal areas, which triggered popular support for Brexit. Leave voters in these communities voted to reject a failing national growth model, in perverse alliance with elites interested solely in preserving it.

Britain's geographical inequalities are chronic, but not inevitable, and should not be a source of despair. Addressing them will not require closing the country off from the global economy, making London poorer, or dismantling the finance sector. Moreover, many of the left's traditional instruments for managing capitalism have been largely devised without reference to geographical inequalities. There are few reasons to assume, for instance, that the renationalisation of some industries by central government would in itself make much difference (although this is not to discount the value of public ownership more generally).

We must also avoid the fatalistic temptation of a universal basic income. Some form of citizens' income may have a role in alleviating poverty, but may at the same time lock in geographical inequalities in earnings. The idea is focused only on our ability to consume, rather than our capacity to produce, and may therefore reinforce key elements of the pre-crisis national growth model.

We certainly do, however, need a rapid reorientation of British economic statecraft if the household income gap between London, the south-east and the rest is to be closed. The twin regional policy strategies of the Conservative and coalition governments in office since 2010 – devolution and local growth – have both failed.

The governance of economic development in the English regions is, frankly, dysfunctional. The recent introduction of new institutional layers from the top down has added complexity to an already overcrowded governance system, which now lacks coherence in terms of strategic co-ordination, planning and funding. Devo-deals at present are little more than partnerships between national and local elites, with few new powers on offer. Meanwhile the democratic accountability of most metro-mayors remains questionable.

Even where metro-mayors might start to work effec-tively, as central funding is funnelled through mayoral offices, the areas without this new model – likely to be more disadvantaged – risk being further marginalised. Moves towards making all local authorities more depend-ent on the taxes they raise locally will only reinforce the structural disadvantage of many regions – with inno-vation in tax policies stymied by new layers of central government conditionality.

The government's recently announced industrial strategy has given greater prominence to 'place' as a pillar of productivity growth. There is now recognition that more resources, rather than clever rhetoric, are required to build regional powerhouses.

But the resources in question remain meagre. Amid a flurry of 'grand challenges' and 'sector deals', the industrial strategy remains largely blind to the actual economic geography of Britain. It downplays enormous infrastructure gaps and the limited capacity of most areas to contribute substantially to the high-tech industries that the government most prizes.

There remains far too little attention to how scientific and engineering excellence might translate into local economic strengths, and, importantly, to the very large, labour-intensive service sectors, such as care and retail, in which most people outside London and the south-east work. We need to think about how these industries can absorb innovation just as much as how to engender new innovation in high-tech industries.

The advocates of urban agglomeration – the highly contested epistemology which underpins the government's fixation on city-led growth – have too often overlooked the role of the public sector in sustaining successful cities, and been too quick to assume that 'what works' in one area can be replicated universally.

When crudely applied, agglomeration counts only local output growth as a measure of success – marginalising the needs of the less productive economic spaces (such as high streets and public parks) which actually enable cities to function. It also brackets off the significant inequalities which have characterised post-industrialism. The juxtaposition of extreme wealth and poverty evident in London is being imported to, for instance, Manchester – with a massive increase in homelessness merely the most obvious symptom.

This wilful blindness to inequality within localities has cultural implications too: witness the high-profile, yet depressingly myopic, opposition to Sheffield's residential tree replacement programme orchestrated by the city's most affluent suburbs, while public services are decimated and trees replaced without controversy) in most of the city. Deindustrialisation has made the vast majority of Sheffield – let alone the wider city-region – largely invisible to its more urbane inhabitants. But cities like Sheffield will not prosper over the long-term unless its poorer areas are benefiting equally from local growth.

So, how can we kick-start sustainable economic development in Britain's disadvantaged regions so that family incomes can start to catch up? Any progressive agenda must be prefaced by much better data on how local economies actually function, with greater analytical capacity within local authorities in this regard. I would then point to five key shifts required.

First, the other UBI: **universal basic infrastructure**. No part of Britain should be held back by deficiencies in the hard and soft infrastructures required to support productive activities. This means, for instance, a fairer regional distribution of transport investment, and an end to broadband blackspots. But it also means access to world-class public services wherever you live in Britain.

Second, **a new settlement between central and local government**. This would encompass the extensive devolution of economic powers to local authorities, including powers to ensure firms with a large local footprint operate in the best interests of the local economy. And if a challenge-based industrial strategy is to work, why not allow local and regional authorities to provide *national* leadership for addressing a particular challenge? A new settlement would also mean, crucially, better representation for regions within the machinery of Whitehall and Westminster.

Even without constitutional change, there is more that local and regional authorities can do to support income growth in their economies. For instance, and third, **local authorities can use their own purchasing power** – and direct that of locally rooted employers, or 'anchors' – to encourage suppliers to create quality career progression opportunities for their workforces, provide support to the voluntary and community sector, and invest in local supply chain development. More effort to democratise local decision-making would also start to address the disconnection many people feel between their lives and how their communities are governed.

Fourth, while, as noted above, local authorities can seek to support local supply chains, **supporting supply chain development in new manufacturing industries** must become a major national policy priority. Manufacturing is essential for enabling productivity growth across all sectors, and in the context of Brexit, it is more vital than ever that Britain is able to nurture the kind of local economic conditions that make the country an attractive place to establish large-scale production facilities. It is only through supply chain development that the government's commitment to advanced manufacturing will create better jobs throughout the country on a meaningful scale.

Of course, any industrial or regional strategy based largely on maximising the benefits on advanced manufacturing, or even high-value service industries, would be too narrowly constituted. We need to develop a much broader conception of how capitalism is embedded in society, by fifth, **strengthening the 'everyday' or 'foundational' economy**.

It is in the foundation economy – spanning the public and private sectors – where the basic needs of society are met: providing care, producing food, maintaining the lived environment (both personal and public spaces), enabling mobility, etc. Such activities are not the source of major productivity improvements – but nor should they be. We certainly need to consider how to disseminate innovation into these areas, but for the purpose of improving resilience rather than profitability per se.

In the relative absence of high-growth industries, life in most local economies is more shaped by conditions in the foundational economy than is the case in London and the south-east. Yet while the foundational economy is place-dependent, it is not place-specific: it is in every place, driven by fairly constant basic needs. Given that many millions of people work in the foundational economy, better management of the relevant industries could have a transformative impact on livelihoods in Britain, especially among the working class – in terms of job security, as well as pay.

Furthermore, solid foundations help to build individual and social capabilities too, in service of the whole economy – thus the conceptual link between universal basic infrastructure and the foundational economy. Not everywhere can expect to become a national centre or global mega-city. But we can get the basics right in every place.

Capitalism ran aground in 2008, nowhere more so than in Britain. Too much of what has passed for radical reform since the crisis has been characterised by pre-crisis intellectual paradigms. To close the regional gap in family incomes, we need to embrace a more grounded capitalism. This means, at a basic level, the recognition that capitalism needs to be managed strategically if it is to develop sustainably – this is the quintessential tenet of industrial strategy, to which the British state remains resistant.

But a grounded capitalism also means recognising its inherent spatiality, and dependence on a seemingly mundane set of locally embedded economic activities which sustain the social and civic life upon which higher-value economic processes depends. We should of course seek to improve

23

wages and conditions in the less glamorous parts of our economy for reasons of economic justice. It will have greatest impact in the most disadvantaged regions. But economic expediency demands exactly the same: nurturing the foundational economy will enable growth everywhere.

3: THE EVERYDAY ECONOMY:
A NEW SETTLEMENT FOR WORK AND PLACE

Rachel Reeves

The UK needs an industrial strategy which prioritises wages and productivity in key parts of the 'everyday economy' and a redistribution of power from capital to labour, through new models of ownership, labour solidarity and worker participation. Local and regional institutions could help ensure thriving, inclusive economies across the country.

We are rightly incensed by endless stories of stagnant wages, in-work poverty, the excesses of platforms like Uber, the poor standards and surveillance culture of companies like Sports Direct, and even the prospect of an automated future that makes work a thing of the past.

But Labour cannot forget that work is essential to its purpose and to its ability to appeal to an electorate divided by class, age, geography and education.[1] As research by the Fabian Society's own Changing Work Centre showed, the majority of people still enjoy their jobs.[2] We need more good jobs and that should be at the heart of Labour's economic policy. Good work sustains us by helping us meet our material needs, and creates a sense of belonging, respect and self-esteem. Work is good.

But with real household incomes on course to be lower in 2022 than in 2008, and with the last decade having seen a proliferation of problems linked to poor pay and working conditions and insecure work, it is clear that the left needs a transformative agenda for the world of work. If an incoming Labour government has one fundamental task it will be to take on these problems at root and ensure the availability of good work: well-paid, but also guaranteeing people the voice, autonomy, flexibility and security they want and should be able to expect.

This is not a question of living standards in isolation. The need to ensure sustainable growth in wages is central to any agenda to get us out of our current economic malaise. For years now, the British economy has depended more and more on ballooning household debt to finance consumption and growth, as wages have stagnated and inequality has widened. The political economist Colin Crouch argues that household debt has underpinned a kind of 'privatised Keynesianism', whereby households take on debt to make up for shortfalls in demand.[3]

Given that debt has been shown to increase the volatility of our economy and the depth of likely downturns, getting household incomes up is also a question of getting our entire economy onto a firmer footing. The question of household incomes is therefore not simply one of improving living standards, but of creating a stable foundation for the living standards we currently have.

Work and wages in the everyday economy

In November 2017, the government published its long awaited industrial strategy White Paper. Perhaps Theresa May's most eye-catching message when she moved into 10 Downing Street was the promise to support the 'just about managing'. I was therefore concerned and disappointed that the industrial strategy had very little to say about those parts of our economy which are characterised by large numbers of employees with low pay. Unfortunately, this has been characteristic of UK industrial policy, which has privileged high-tech manufacturing industries and done too little to address productivity and pay in the areas of the economy where the biggest gains might be made, and which – when they have paid attention to place at all – have preferred working with local enterprise partnerships than with elected local authorities.

While the White Paper promised the creation of 'sector deals', the substance of such deals was left unexplained, and the focus for those initial deals was on life sciences, construction, artificial intelligence and automotives. These areas might offer GDP growth but with the exception of construction they employ relatively small numbers of workers, many of whom are high-skilled, with high levels of productivity. Apart from construction, they are also concentrated in London and the south-east.

We need to put an equal emphasis on the 'everyday economy' – those sectors characterised by high levels of employment and generally low levels of pay and productivity, which sustain all our daily lives and on which we depend for healthy, happy, functioning communities. This includes retail, the utilities, health and social care. Significantly, these are also sectors which employ a disproportionate share of Britain's female workforce.

If Labour is to put forward an agenda able to improve living standards for the many, then it must champion an industrial strategy guided first and foremost by what is going on in the everyday economy. But what does this mean in practice?

An industrial strategy for the everyday economy

The Fabian Society's retail taskforce, which reported in 2017, made an extremely valuable contribution in this respect,

27

offering a rich array of ideas for improving skills and management and for greater representation of the needs of workers and communities within the retail sector.[4] Ideas like a Catapult Centre for management and a 'super skills council' for the retail industry are promising, as is the call for collaboration between business and local authorities to produce local retail plans. The work of John Lewis chair Charlie Mayfield, as a part of the Productivity Leadership Group, could also be transformative if it focuses on those low productivity, high employment parts of our economy.

Individual policies like these, for improving productivity and wages in the everyday economy, should be underpinned by a nation-wide strategy for good work. This could be driven by a widened remit for the Low Pay Commission and through brokering dialogue between employers and workers in the sectors that comprise the everyday economy. Sector deals could form a key part of this good work strategy. Helping our firms drive up productivity is one of the key ingredients to improving wages, and this will be a key aspect of sector deals. Ensuring better access to finance for small and medium enterprises across all parts of the country is essential to this. A network of regional banks, perhaps in line with the German *Sparkassen*, which I visited five years ago, could ultimately address this problem. Meanwhile, a national infrastructure bank, along the lines of the green investment bank but in public ownership, might be charged with ensuring we have world-class infrastructure.

However, if we are to ensure that productivity gains are shared in terms of higher pay, workers must be given a central role, on company boards as well as in conversations about changes to working practice and the integration of new technology. As Nita Clarke of the Involvement and Participation Association argues, improved worker voice can benefit firms by boosting productivity. All too often, staff find their abilities underutilised because they are not listened to by employers. Sometimes organisations do not even manage to explain their purpose to their people.[5] All of this serves to harm motivation among staff and deprive employers of the input of motivated workers whose day-to-day experience gives them huge insight into what works – and what doesn't – for the firm.

Place and procurement

An industrial strategy able to tackle wages will also need to have a sensitivity to place. It is worrying that, despite an emphasis on place, there is little attention to local democracy within the industrial strategy White Paper.[6] There is a strong correlation in Britain between levels of pay and productivity, on the one hand, and geography, on the other. While national government can play a part in ensuring that investment in infrastructure and public services is spread more equally across the country, powerful, local democratic institutions will be absolutely key to any strategy which seeks to address stagnant family incomes in many struggling parts of the country.

Preston City Council, working with the Manchester-based Centre for Local Economic Strategies, have set a powerful example by working with local 'anchor institutions' to strengthen their local economy. These institutions – like universities, schools, hospitals and large businesses with roots in the community – are key because they are large employers who spend a large amount on procurement with their supply chain, and because they are unlikely to relocate due to historic ties and relationships in the local area. In Preston, the council has worked with these institutions to maximise the amount they spend on procurement in the local community, boosting local small businesses and even supporting the creation of local cooperatives. Equally, there is immense potential for local government and anchor institutions to forge living wage deals to drive up pay in an area. A unit for local wealth building based in 10 Downing Street, under the authority of the prime minister, could create a national economic plan to build local capacity and organise the cross-departmental collaboration necessary for its implementation. Regional banks would, again, be key to this agenda of enabling autonomous institutions for the kind of inclusive, local wealth building we need.

Solidarity in a changing economy

Driving much of the decline in the labour share of Britain's wealth – down by around 5 per cent since the 1970s – has been the decline of the power of organised labour. Gavin Kelly and Dan Tomlinson of the Resolution Foundation warn that we are on course for as few as one in five employees to be a trade union member by 2030. This trend is driven by deep-rooted factors including the long-term collapse of heavy industry in Britain, the rise of smaller businesses and self-employment, the impact of austerity on public sector employment, changing social attitudes and the most restrictive trade-union legislation in Europe.[7]

It is important for Labour to not just improve wages in the short term, but to entrench a fairer settlement around workers' wages and conditions for the long term. That means we require a strong, autonomous institutional infrastructure able to withstand a hostile Conservative government. The GMB is already doing good work, fighting for Uber drivers and others in the platform economy in court, while Community has set a promising example by supporting shared workspaces and offering a range of logistical support for the self-employed.

But central government can take on a much more active supporting role. The next Labour government must provide financial and institutional support for the institutions we need to entrench a fairer balance of power for labour, in relation to management and shareholders. There are myriad examples of these ventures from around the world. For instance, the SMart cooperative in Belgium, which is comprised of self-employed workers. It deals with their clients (including platforms like Deliveroo) on their behalf, and also provides access to advice, workspace, training, business support and insurance.[8] Meanwhile, in the United States, websites like HourVoice and Shyft are attempts to redress the imbalance of control, information and coordination between precarious workers, employers and platforms. As the shadow chancellor John McDonnell has argued, Labour in central and local government should be championing alternative models of ownership, which can guarantee workers not only greater say over decisions made in their workplace, but also a greater share of the profits.[9]

The introduction of the minimum wage and tax credits were some of the proudest achievements of the last Labour government. Protecting them both – and universal credit – from Tory cuts is hugely important. But incomes cannot be raised by the state alone, and a key test for Labour at all levels of government will be in our willingness to give power away and our ability to collaborate with, and empower, other stakeholders and institutions to create the conditions for higher incomes and a fairer distribution of wealth within companies. In this chapter, I have begun to sketch out the institutions and principles which can underlie a new, fairer settlement around work and wages: an industrial strategy which prioritises wages and productivity in the key sectors of the everyday economy; a redistribution of power from capital to labour, through new models of ownership, labour solidarity and worker participation; and local and regional institutions with the capabilities to ensure thriving, inclusive economies across the country.

4: BUILDING ON SUCCESS: LABOUR MARKET REFORMS TO GET BRITAIN EARNING MORE

Torsten Bell

To boost household incomes we need to increase how much people work and how much they are paid. There have been big successes in labour market policy in recent decades but huge failures too. So while we now have higher employment levels and higher hourly pay for the lowest earners, we still need to tackle major challenges including insecure work, weak bargaining power and poor pay progression.

Lots of things matter for family incomes – but for British households as a whole nothing matters as much as the labour market. Questions of who has a job and what they get paid for doing it might not be the only determinant of our living standards – but they are certainly the first. So what would it take for Britain's labour market to do a better job of driving up our living standards?

Let's start with the lessons of recent years of what has worked – and what has been a disaster. On the positive side, over the last two decades Britain has been following a labour market policy with twin objectives: higher employment levels and higher pay for the lowest earners. On both counts, with ups and down, it has seen big successes. Employment levels and our minimum wage now stand at record highs – 75.2 per cent of adults aged 16 to 64 are working (Q4 2017) and the wage floor is £7.83 per hour (from 1 April 2018 for those 25 years or over).

In the second half of the 1990s, following the disaster of 3 million unemployed after the recessions of the 1980s and 1990s, there came a renewed focus on employment levels as a key objective of public policy. And a new policy approach was shaped to achieve it. This combined increased incentives to work (via tax credits) and expectations of work, alongside greater support to help make it happen (with childcare for example). In big picture terms this combination worked, in some cases dramatically so. Worklessness, which was a national disaster in the 1990s, has shrunk throughout the last two decades from being the experience of over 1 in 5 working-age households to just 1 in 7 in Q4 2017.

Employment rates matter so much for living standards not just because they drive how many people get paid but also who those people are. What matters is not just the overall level of employment income but the distribution of it. Degree educated, white, prime-age (30–49) men are almost always in work wherever they live in the country and however good or badly the economy is doing. It is not these groups that benefit most from the tighter labour market that higher employment brings, but those nearer to the edge of the labour market – the employment rates of older workers, mothers, ethnic minorities and people with disabilities vary hugely across time and place. For instance the employment rate for people with disabilities is 49 per cent in the south-east compared to 36 per cent on Tyneside, and while single parents in South Yorkshire and inner London now have similar rates of employment the pace of improvement has been very different. Lone parent employment increased by 20 percentage points in inner London over the past seven years compared to half that in South Yorkshire where the labour market has been weaker.

In general the rise in employment among single parents was an undercelebrated triumph of the pre-2010 Labour government. There was a transformational increase in employment from 43 per cent in 1996 to 54 per cent on the eve of the financial crisis. This was part of the reason why lone parent households' income levels increased 1.6 times faster than working-age households as a whole between the mid-1990s and the financial crisis.

Further increases in employment levels in the last few years have disproportionately benefited lower income families – almost all of the employment growth in Britain since the financial crisis has taken place amongst the poorest third of families. This is predistribution in action.

Figure 1: Employment rates by decile of the equivalised net household income distribution

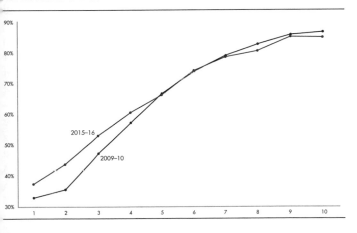

Notes: Households are included in this analysis if they contain at least one adult aged 16–69.
Source: Resolution Foundation analysis of Family Resources Survey

Meanwhile, on the second pillar of labour market policy over the last two decades, the introduction and ramping up of the minimum wage has been perhaps the most high-profile way in which government policy has directly increased family living standards via the labour market. And it has been a triumph, without the significant employment losses that its opponents predicted. The early years of the minimum wage from 1999 saw the abolition of extremes of low pay (in 1998, 7 per cent of the workforce were earning below half of typical hourly pay, in 2002 it was 5 per cent and in 2005 2.5 per cent). The big hikes that have followed the introduction of the national living wage more recently lie behind the biggest single-year reduction in low pay in 40 years (5.1 million employees were low paid in 2016, down from 5.4 million in 2015). The lowest paid workers are currently receiving the highest wage increases in Britain – and that is likely to continue to be the case until the national living wage reaches its target level of 60 per cent of median earnings in 2020.

Figure 2: Growth in real hourly earnings (excluding overtime)

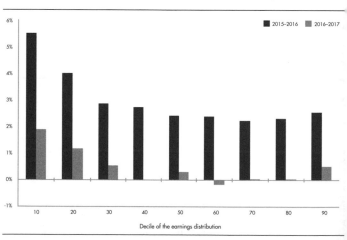

Source: Resolution Foundation analysis, Annual Survey of Hours and Earnings

It's clear that the policy focus on full employment and low pay has brought rewards. But recent experience has more to teach us than that. We need to reflect on what has gone wrong, not just what has gone right. Britain's households are after all in the middle of what is projected to be a full 17-year pay squeeze, with earnings not set to return to their pre-crisis levels until 2025. Recent years have also seen big increases in insecure work, with 900,000 workers now on zero-hours contracts.

Figure 3: Average annual employee earnings, CPI-adjusted: outturn and successive OBR projections (Q4 2016 prices)

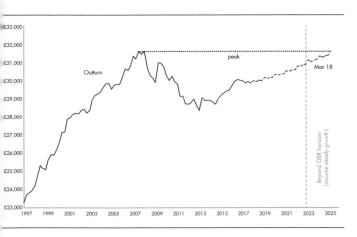

Source: Resolution Foundation analysis, OBR

In particular anyone thinking about the future of labour market policy needs to ask why the financial crisis caused not only a huge pay squeeze, but a very swift one. It's always been obvious that over the long term how much we produce for the work we do matters a lot for our pay, but one of the big lessons of the last decade is that some economic shocks can feed through very quickly indeed into our wages. In cases where Britain is either the only country affected by a shock (Brexit) or particularly hard hit (the financial crisis), the swift hit to living standards is driven by a falling exchange rate and the higher (import-driven) inflation that follows. In a flexible labour market, and in the absence of strong trade unions demanding that wages keep pace with fast-rising prices, big falls in real pay result. This is the dynamic behind pay declining by 5.3 per cent after the financial crisis and the return of shrinking pay packets in 2017. It was something no-one expected when the crisis hit in 2008 but which, now that we have experienced it twice in quick succession, should be front of mind for policy makers.

Another lesson from the financial crisis is the degree to which more insecure, atypical forms of work dominated post-crisis jobs growth. Self-employment has accounted for around 30 per cent of the employment growth since the crisis, while between 2011 and 2016 we saw an additional 130,000 agency workers. Importantly, though the growth in such work has now largely ceased (another benefit of a high employment and tightening labour market) the level remains too high. Yes, many enjoy the flexibility of non-traditional work, but collectively we should still be concerned about the pay penalties and lack of employment protection that too often come alongside such work.

Where do these labour market lessons of recent history leave us? Should a forward-looking labour market agenda simply double down on what has worked in the past and avoid the things that have gone, so badly, wrong?

Well yes on the avoiding mistakes part – we could really do with a growing economy that avoids UK-specific policy driven economic shocks. And we should ignore some misplaced recent arguments that claim our individual pay packets have become entirely and permanently disconnected from the nation's gross domestic product – productivity and growth really matter for our living standards. We also need to recognise that during any future economic shocks we should be paying more attention to the exchange rate, not because we are holiday makers but because we are workers.

And yes we should retain and build on progress on high employment and low pay. But crucially now is the time to update our approach, because a 21st century labour market policy should reflect the reality of the 21st century labour market not that of the 1990s.

On employment, we need to avoid going backwards on some big wins. That's why elements of universal credit (as it is currently planned) that weaken work incentives for second earners and single parents are unwise, not least because these are the groups most responsive to such incentives.

And while overall employment is at record highs, a new policy focus should recognise that there remain places and groups with far too low employment rates. Birmingham, for example, stands out for very low employment levels – 61 per cent, which is 15 percentage points lower than Bristol just 90 miles away. That is a disgrace from the perspective of economic output and distribution. National policy alone can't solve these huge regional differences, so we need a new focus where the role of geography and local economic leadership takes centre stage.

Our approach to those with a disability also needs a revolution. We need to prioritise supporting people to stay in work when they become ill rather than simply testing them for fitness for work once they have dropped out. Doing so would help close the disability employment gap which at 28 percentage points is far higher than the EU average of 20 points.

But, while targeting high employment remains key, policy needs to shift to confront new challenges. Worklessness is no longer the stand-out feature of our labour market as it was in the 1980s and 1990s. New challenges have emerged and just as we developed an active labour market policy agenda to confront the old challenges, we should do the same again today. People today are largely in work, but too many are insecure and too many are stuck.

The good news is that a time of high employment is exactly the right moment to strengthen the regulation of our labour market. There is no reason why it should be legal to leave people on a zero-hours contract when they are working regular hours. The law should explicitly protect anyone who chooses not to accept extra hours from being disadvantaged. The tax system should not be offering firms big incentives to try to argue that their workforce are in fact self-employed. More radically we should be exploring ways to require firms that extensively rely on non-contracted hours to pay more for the privilege so that the benefits of flexibility go two ways. We used to call it overtime.

Reducing insecurity in these ways is necessary anyway because some practices are simply not defensible. But it is also essential for living standards because for too many workers, and especially the young, a feeling of insecurity is holding them back from doing something too much of Britain has forgotten how to do: ask for a pay rise. Unions of course are also part of the answer to that challenge. The good news is public attitudes, especially amongst the young, are positive – only 8 per cent of millennials are opposed to unions in principal.[10] The bad news is that young people outside the public sector generally have very little concept of what unions can do for them, beyond seeing membership as individual insurance against particularly bad treatment at work. Giving unions access to workplaces to overcome he awareness gap would be a good start. And the degree o which young voters have more positive attitudes towards unions should encourage politicians to look again at ludicrous bits of anti-union rules – like the ban on electronic balloting – and to institutionally build in more opportunities for workers voices to be heard. Well supported workers should be sitting on company boards, and at a sectoral level we should also be building on the tripartite success of the Low Pay Commission and the recent government decision o give the TUC and CBI strategic oversight of the national retraining scheme. We also need to celebrate the success of unions that are innovating and engaging with technologies that can help redefine collective action, while recognising that overall far too little of such innovation is taking place.

As with employment, on low pay we need to keep doing what has worked. We should press ahead with the rapid increases in the national living wage up to 2020, but the next step after that should be taking stock of what that huge rise between 2016 and 2020 has done to our labour market, for example what the side effects have been of moving from 7 per cent to 14 per cent of the workforce relying on the legal minimum. We may be able to go further; there is after all little strong evidence on where exactly the limit is for raising the minimum wage without significant side-effects. But there will be a limit, so any changes should be done in a steady and planned manner with our eyes open to the evidence. We should also look to reduce the number of age bands for the minimum wage, in the first instance by bringing down the age of entitlement to the national living wage below 25.

But our approach to low pay, upon which the UK economy has become far too reliant, also needs to broaden to recognise the nature of the challenges we face today. An approach limited to simply pulling ever harder on one lever, the minimum wage, is insufficient. There are three new frontiers in the fight against low pay that should be explored First, hours worked are as important as the hourly wage in determining low paid workers living standards, but never get talked about. Indeed falls in the hours worked by low paid men have exerted an upward pressure on inequality since the 1990s. Second, while the minimum wage has helped reduce the depth of low pay, it has (until recently) left the breadth of it far too high. That is to say it can narrow the gap between middle earners and the bottom, but not address the structural factors that leave more workers on low pay in the UK than in many other developed countries. To deal with that challenge we need to talk about progression routes out of low-paid work and the productivity of low-paid sectors of our economy. The challenge is big: fewer than one in 20 people who were sales assistants back in 2011, for example, had moved up to become retail managers or supervisors five years later. Third, we need to explore in more detail whether in some parts of the country low-paid workers have too little power in the labour market because they have no meaningful choice of employer. This so-called monopsony problem has the potential to be a big drag on wages and is driving a big debate in the US that is sadly missing on this side of the Atlantic.

Along with the shifts in approach above, a full strategy to boost living standards through the labour market needs to recognise not just the need to raise productivity of the firms and workers we already have, but that we have slowed our pace of human capital improvement – that is to say we are not getting better qualified at the rate we once were. It would also note that the public sector pay restraint of recent years has reached the end of the road, and that much more needs to be done to close gender pay gaps that drag on women's earnings.

So stepping back, a balanced reading of history tells us that labour market policy has seen big successes in recent decades but huge failures too. We need to recognise both – continuing with what worked, avoiding what didn't – and update our approach for the new challenges that 21st century Britain faces. That is the key to ensuring the labour market does what it in the end exists for: improving the living standards of the working people of Britain.

5: WIN-WIN: HOW TACKLING INEQUALITY IMPROVES GROWTH AND DISTRIBUTION

Özlem Onaran and Alexander Guschanski

Tackling inequality is 'win-win'. A more equal economy will bring stronger, more stable growth and it will direct more of the nation's prosperity into the hands of ordinary families. While national income has more than doubled over the last 40 years, low income households have been left behind. Now even institutions like the IMF and OECD are calling for governments to reduce inequality as a strategy for growth.

Why did living standards of most households grow only slowly while national income has more than doubled in the last 40 years? How are these trends related to rising income inequality? Are these unavoidable outcomes in the age of automation and the gig economy or can we design economic policies to reverse these trends? What would be the impact of increasing equality on employment and economic growth? In this article we tackle these questions, relying on our recent research at the Greenwich Political Economy Research Centre.

Why do most working people feel left behind?

Over the last 40 years overall national income has been growing, but working people have not been getting their fair share.

The income available to the 'average' household in Britain[11] has more than doubled since 1977.[12] On average

45

we have more than twice as much income than our parents. This prompts the following question: why does it appear to working people that they are not better off, and in most cases worse off than the previous generations? To answer this, we must look at trends which, until recently, remained largely unacknowledged by neoliberal economists and policy makers. First, the share of 'poor' people[13] has increased by staggering 40 per cent in Britain in this period. Second, the share of national income held by the top 1 per cent has more than doubled.[14] While the overall pie has been growing, most of us have not been getting our fair share. The 'great recession' and Brexit exacerbated these trends, with real pay still lower compared to its peak in early 2008 in Britain, following the longest and most dramatic period of declining real wages since Victorian times.

One way to understand these diverging trends is by investigating changes in the wage share (the share of labour compensation in national income). Most people depend on wage income, while income from dividends or owning a business mostly accrues to the top earners. Put differently, wages are more equally distributed than income from profits. Therefore, a decline in the wage share usually means that those in the lower income groups are losing out with respect to high-income households. The last four decades have been characterised by a drastic fall in the wage share in both OECD and emerging economies. In Britain the wage share fell from 74.1 per cent of national income in 1975 to 66.8 per cent in 2017.[15] Importantly, the fall in the wage share has been borne by those earning median wages and below, while managerial salaries for those at the very top have raced upward. People on average and low wages have effectively been hit twice, having access to a shrinking slice of a progressively smaller wage pie.

Why did the wage share decline?

The changes in bargaining power between capital and labour have been the main reason behind these trends. There have been dramatic socio-economic changes in the past decades, in particular:

- technological change, specifically the increasing use of robotics and information and communication technology;
- the rise of global value chains between advanced and emerging economies, with important development such as the entrance of China into the WTO as well as increasing migration;
- the rising importance of 'shareholder value' orientation and short-termism in determining management behaviour, and
- changes in the institutional framework in which bargaining takes place, including a sharp decline in union density and collective bargaining coverage in all OECD countries, with the highest decline taking place in Britain.

In our work we have analysed the impact of these factors on the wage share in different industries in 14 OECD countries including Britain.[16] Our findings suggest that changes in bargaining power explain more than half of the decline in the labour share. This decline is primarily related to a strong deterioration in union density and retrenchment of the welfare state. Conventional wisdom often focuses on migration as the most important consequence of globalisation for the rise in inequality. In contrast, offshoring – the relocation of production to low-wage countries, rather than migration – is the most important driver of the negative impact of globalisation according to our findings. Technological change has a negative effect due to the automation of routine tasks; however, it does not alone explain the strong decline in the

47

wage share, specifically not for low-skilled workers. Instead our findings suggest that labour has not benefited as much as capital from the technological advancements due to the decline in workers' bargaining power. The increase in female employment in the absence of strong collective representation of women and the enforcement of equal pay legislation also contributes to the fall in the labour share. Lastly we also found a negative effect of the 'shareholder value' orientation and increasing financial overhead costs and subsequent wage suppression on the labour share in Britain.[17]

How can we reverse inequality?

Setting up institutions for a level playing field is the key to reversing inequality. Bargaining relations are determined by institutions and policies and can be altered to offset the negative impact of technological change and globalisation on inequality. The negative effects of openness or global integration are not an unavoidable destiny, but rather an outcome of current domestic and international policies, including persistent austerity, and precarious employment practices in the name of labour market flexibility. Tackling income inequality requires a restructuring of the institutional and policy framework in which wage bargaining takes place and ensuring that the bargaining power of labour is more in balance with that of capital.

Specifically, the impact of globalisation or technological change is likely to be significantly moderated and/or offset by:

● stronger bargaining power of labour via an improvement in union legislation, by re-regulating the labour market, banning zero-hours contracts, widening collective bargaining and ensuring an active role for the state in institution building to facilitate sectoral bargaining structures;

- increasing statutory minimum wages and putting processes in place for the incremental increase of minimum wage to the level of a living wage; expediting this process through the use of public contracts;
- improving and enforcing equal pay legislation and women's representation in collective bargaining;
- increasing the social wage via higher public spending in public services and social security, ending public sector pay freezes, restoring and strengthening the welfare state
- re-orientating macroeconomic policies towards ensuring full employment in order to rebalance both power relations and the structure of the economy;
- supporting job creation and restructuring with a large public investment programme centred on physical investments and social infrastructure;
- enforcing pay ratios via public procurement criteria between top pay and lowest paid at companies to moderate high pay;
- substantially shortening working time in parallel with the historical growth in productivity with wage compensation at least for those earning below median income;
- implement appropriately designed taxation and corporate governance that create incentives to decrease dividend payments and share buybacks and increase wages in line with productivity growth, including higher taxation of dividend payments and capital gains, and prohibition of share buybacks; decoupling executives' remuneration from share prices; including representatives of employees and the wider public on company boards.

Arguably, the recent rise in political populism – ranging from Brexit to Trump to nationalism in continental Europe – is partly a response to increasing inequality. Instead of holding the main drivers of inequality identified in our analysis responsible, the blame is often put on migrants as they constitute an easy target: they are visible, while socio-economic processes such as financialisation and offshoring are more elusive. Our research suggests that populist strategies will not lead to any improvements in equality but might rather decrease labour's bargaining power by distracting from the actual institutional factors behind the fall in the wage share.

What would increasing equality mean for economic growth and productivity?

Our research shows that this policy package would create a win-win situation, characterised by a radically fairer society and increased economic growth.[18] The decline in the wage share in GDP has gone along with weaker growth in output over the last three decades. The seemingly higher growth rates of 2000–07 in Britain appear, with hindsight, as a mirage: in the absence of strong productivity-oriented wage increases, rising household debt was the fuel for consumption. This proved to be a fragile growth model that collapsed in the 'great recession'. The weak recovery in Britain with the lowest growth rate in the G7 recently is also built on the same shaky foundations – household debt.

Neoliberal economic policy has seen wages as costs to businesses. When the wage share is lower, profits are higher. As a result, the usual assumption is that when the wage share falls, and the profit share increases, growth will be boosted; investment by firms will pick up, and exports will become more competitive thanks to lower labour costs. This thinking guides policies which promote wage moderation in Britain and is responsible for the promotion of practices such as zero-hour contracts in the name of labour market flexibility. But neoliberal economists fail to explain the persistence of declining labour shares and falling growth rates in the UK, and most other major economies.

The answer lies in the other side to this story: wages are not merely an economic cost detracted from company profits, but the source of demand in the economy. As the majority of middle- and low-income people depend on wages, an increase in the wage share implies a redistribution of income from high-income households to middle- and low-income households, who spend a larger share of their income than people at the top. Therefore, an increase in the wage share will increase household spending, and as such generate demand for firms and stimulate their investment.

Wages play a dual role in the economy: rising wages are both a cost to employers and a potential source for new sales – they cut into profits and yet can boost them. Whether the negative effect of a lower wage share on consumption or the positive effect on investment and net exports is larger is an empirical question that will depend on how the structure of an economy such as the difference in the propensity to consume out of wage and profit income, the sensitivity of investment to sales versus profitability, the impact of labour costs on prices, labour intensity of production, sensitivity of exports and imports to domestic prices relative to foreign prices, and the importance of foreign markets relative to the size of the economy. Since either situation is possible in theory, the impact is an empirical question.

Recent research indicates that in Britain the positive effects of an increase in the wage share outweigh any negative consequences on business profits or exports; Britain grows faster with more not less equality – in the terminology it is a 'wage-led' economy.[19]

The negative effect of inequality on growth is also confirmed by recent research at international organisations such as the OECD and the IMF.[20] The IMF, after promoting 'trickle down economics' for several decades, recently became outspoken about the negative impact of personal income inequality on growth. However, their focus lies on only personal income distribution, and neglects the inequality between labour and capital. Moreover, the effects work only over longer periods of time. For example, they link increasing inequality to lower growth via a worsening of access to education for low-income households, growing trade imbalances and a higher probability of financial crises.

In contrast, the positive effect of higher equality – higher wage share – on demand, as emphasised by our research, could boost growth immediately and shows the importance of demand effects of wages.

The impact of increasing the wage share is amplified when combined with a policy of progressive taxation and public investment. Our economic modelling indicates that a 1 percentage point increase in the wage share, combined with an increase in public spending of 1 per cent of GDP (about £20bn per year), an increase in the average tax rate on capital of one per cent and a cut in the average tax rate on labour income of 1 per cent would lead to an increase in GDP by 3.37 per cent.[21] Private investment increases as well since public investment complements private investment; expectations of future sales, rather than immediate profits boosts investment and higher wages stimulate productivity. The public budget balance also improves thanks to higher growth and tax revenues.

The effects are significantly larger if we take the behaviour of our trade partners into account. The positive impacts of a declining wage share that in theory arise from increasing export competitiveness disappear if all countries make the same cuts together in a 'beggar thy neighbour' fashion. This has characterised the last four decades and the domestic repression of demand has dominated the outcome in each country including the UK. We have strong empirical evidence to conclude that Britain and the EU as a whole are wage-led and would therefore vastly benefit from a simultaneous increase in the wage share.[22]

Conclusion

Overall income has been growing but working people have not been getting their fair share. While incomes at the bottom have declined, incomes at the top have continued to increase. This trend is reflected in a declining wage share. Our research shows that changes in the bargaining power between capital and labour, rather than the unavoidable consequences of technological change and globalisation are behind this trend. Consequently, it is in our hands to set a level playing field where the bargaining power of labour is more in balance with that of capital and so to recuperate labour's income share that was lost in the last four decades.

We have strong empirical evidence to conclude that increasing equality would lead to higher growth. The UK is a wage-led economy and consequently the positive effects of a reduction in income inequality outweighs any negative effects. The effect would be even stronger if it is supported by a progressive public policy package and if it happens simultaneously in all EU member states or globally. While a coordinated global boost to wages might appear as wishful thinking, in fact the exact opposite has been happening in the last four decades: the wage share has declined in advanced and emerging economies simultaneously. It is now on us to revert this trend.

This article builds on the results of a project funded by the Institute for New Economic Thinking, as well as two joint projects of FEPS, GPERC, TASC and ECLM.

6: TOO HIGH A PRICE: A MANAGED EXCHANGE RATE FOR EXPORTS, INVESTMENT AND GROWTH

John Mills

The British economy will not grow fast enough to deliver decent increases in household incomes while business investment and exports are so low. UK manufacturing is chronically uncompetitive on world markets because of the exchange rate. Britain must imitate other countries who manage their exchange rate and target a much lower value for sterling if we are to get the economy growing fast enough to increase wages significantly.

Between 2007, the year before the crash, and 2017 the UK economy grew by 11 per cent.[23] During this period our population increased by 8 per cent,[24] reducing the increase in real GDP per head to just under 3 per cent. At the same time, UK real wages have been suppressed further for two reasons – the need to finance our annual balance of payments deficit and the return on capital being higher than economic growth. As a result the wage share of GDP has fallen. What little earnings growth is left has then tended to be scooped up by the most advantaged.

The only significant countervailing factor has been the rise in the proportion of GDP which we consume instead of investing. Capital investment has fallen from 20 per cent of GDP in 2007 to under 16 per cent[25] now, thus providing a significant short-term boost to real disposable incomes – but at the expense of our future. Despite this shift, most of the population have still had no real wage increases for the past 10 years.

The bald fact is that on current policies this situation will inevitably continue. We will never see any sustainable rises in real wages for most people without the economy expanding much faster – at, say, 3 per cent to 4 per cent every year – than it is at present, not least because, as well as increasing wages, we need to invest much more as a percentage of GDP than we do now.

The current consensus is that we are likely to see the UK economy growing over the next few years by no more than an average of between 1.5 per cent and 2 per cent per annum.[26] If the only way to rising living standards for nearly everyone is to get the economy to expand much faster than this, how is this to be done? There is a solution and the starting point is to look at the imbalances from which the UK economy currently suffers.

Investment

To support a reasonable rate of growth the proportion of UK GDP devoted to investment as opposed to consumption, at 15.6 per cent[27], is far too low. The world average is 26 per cent and in China the ratio is not far short of 50 per cent.[28] Furthermore, of the 15.6 per cent, only 12.8 per cent[29] consists of physical assets and of this, only 2.7 per cent[30] goes towards the type of investment – mechanisation, technology and power – from which big increases in output per hour almost uniquely spring. Social investment in roads, rail, schools, hospitals and housing, however desirable, unfortunately – and contrary to widely held opinion – has negligible impact on our growth rate. Private investment in office blocks, new restaurants, or support infrastructure for legal, financial, advertising and other services, does no better. It is in manufacturing, and particularly light industry, that machines, technology and increased use of power find their natural home. By the time the 2.7 per cent of GDP we devote to this type of investment has been offset against the depreciation of similar past investments, nothing is left to build the future.[31] This is arguably by far the most important reason why we have such an acute productivity problem.

Deindustrialisation

Even as late as 1970, about 30 per cent of the UK's GDP came from manufacturing.[32] Now the figure is less than 10 per cent[33] and still drifting down. This has been a disastrous development for three separate reasons. First, productivity increases are much easier to achieve in manufacturing than in services, so we have foregone increases in output per hour and GDP growth which we could have secured if we had looked after our industrial base better. Second, manufacturing pays on average much higher wages – about 20 per cent more[34] – than the average, often providing more satisfying and fulfilling jobs than in services, with much better employment distribution between the regions. Third, well over half our exports are goods rather than services[35] and with our severely weakened industrial base, we do not have enough to sell to the rest of the world to pay for our imports. In 2016 we had a balance of payments deficit on goods of £134bn[36] – nearly 7 per cent of GDP[37] – of which manufacturers alone accounted for £99bn.[38]

Paying our way in the world

Our trade deficit was £41bn in 2016[39], with a substantial £92bn surplus on services[40] going a fair way to offset our £134bn deficit on goods.[41] On its own, an annual deficit of about £40bn might be manageable. Unfortunately our overall balance of payments position which includes the flow of investment income and transfers is in much worse shape – with recent deficits of about £100bn a year.[42] The positive net income from investments abroad which we used to have has now turned into a very substantial deficit – £51bn in 2016 compared to a £7bn surplus as recently as 2011.[43] The main underlying reason for this swing is that every year we have an overall deficit of around £100bn:[44] the lost returns on the assets sold and borrowing required to finance these short-falls adds substantially to our income deficit. Second, our net transfers abroad – net payments to the EU, remittances abroad by immigrants and our aid programmes – have also roughly doubled in recent years – to £22bn[45] in 2016.

Debt

The UK economy is awash with debt. Total borrowing has increased by a staggering 1,480 per cent since 2000.[46] The national debt which had fallen to 25 per cent of GDP in 1992, and was still only 29 per cent in 2002, is now running at 87 per cent.[47] The main reason why debt has risen so rapidly is that balance of payments deficits syphon demand out of the economy, which has to be replaced by unfunded expenditure, if the economy is not drastically to contract. Within any period, all borrowing in the economy between the main sectors – government, consumers, businesses and the foreign balance – has to be exactly matched by lend-ing, and any surpluses have to be matched by deficits. This is why foreign payments deficits have to be matched by government borrowing. One is the mirror image of the other.

Inequality

There are three main axes of inequality all of which have become much greater during the last few decades. These are disparities between the regions of the country, between the generations and between those who are wealthy and those who are not so lucky. It is the collapse of manufacturing which largely explains the gap that there now is between London and the rest of the country. In 2013, gross value added per worker in London was £40,000 compared to £17,000 in Wales.[48] It is lack of housing, suitable education, training and job opportunities which explains why younger people are doing so badly. It is ultra-low interest rates and the consequent asset inflation which mainly explains our increasing wealth and life chance disparities.

Solutions

What can we do to overcome these problems? There is a long list of supply side remedies – on education and training, increased spending on infrastructure, changes to governance, making finance more readily available for investment – broadly favoured by the left and usually rolled into an industrial strategy. There is an equally long list of measures favoured by the right – deregulation, increased competition, lower taxation, privatisation and a smaller state. Neither of these approaches, however, will be successful without tackling the root of the UK's economic malaise because all the remedies favoured by left and right are much more addressed at symptoms than causes of our poor performance. The UK's fundamental problem is that we are chronically uncompetitive on world markets – not on high-tech manufacturing or services both of which are not very price sensitive and where we have natural advantages not available elsewhere – but on run-of-the-mill manufactured goods where pricing is critical and on which maintaining a reasonable foreign payments balance depends.

Why is our manufacturing so uncompetitive? It is no
because machinery, raw materials and components – which
make up about one third of manufacturing costs on average[49] – are any more expensive in the UK than they are
elsewhere. It is because we charge the rest of the world at too
high a rate for the other two-thirds of total costs. Compared
to other countries, Britain is too expensive with respect to
labour and management costs, plus all other overheads –
everything from repairs and maintenance to audit charges,
cleaning costs, travel expenses, plus provisions for interest,
profits and taxation. This is almost entirely an exchange
rate problem.

Figure 1: Chained Real Effective Exchange Rates 1975–2016

Source: International Financial Statistics Yearbooks. Washington DC, IMF. 2000
edition: pages 344 & 345 for China and 980 & 981 for the UK; 2010 edition:
page 229 for China and 744 for the UK; 2017 edition: page 243 for China
and 825 for the UK. Based in all cases on Relative Unit Labour Costs

How did this come about? It is arguable that sterling has been
too strong for nearly all the time since the UK started indus-

rialising but our lack of industrial competitiveness really set
n when monetarism, which morphed into neo-liberalism,
took hold of the economic policy agenda in the late 1970s.
Figure 1 shows what happened. The UK's exchange rate
soared as monetary policy was tightened to combat inflation,
and interest rates were raised peaking with a base rate of 17
per cent in 1980.[50] This situation was made even worse in the
late 1990s and early 2000s when major policy changes[51] made
it exceptionally easy for foreign parties to buy UK assets of
all kinds, causing a huge inflow of capital to the UK. Between
2000 and 2010 net sales of UK portfolio assets – shares in
existing companies, bonds and property but excluding
direct investment in new factories and machinery – totalled
£615bn,[52] a figure equal to about half our annual GDP at the
time.[53] Sterling rose until £1 was worth $2 in 2007[54] as the
UK's manufacturing base collapsed.

This is the situation which we have to reverse if we are
going to get the UK economy to start growing again fast
enough to increase average real wages. Essentially, we need
to get the cost base – the rate at which we charge out all sterling based costs – in the UK down to a level where it is worth
siting production facilities in the UK rather than elsewhere
for the medium- and low-tech manufacturing on which most
world trade depends. And how far would sterling have to
fall to make this possible? Some fairly easy calculations show
that there would need to be roughly parity with the US dollar
and about £1.00 = €0.85 against the euro.[55]

Would it be possible to get sterling down to this level
and to keep it there, to provide the conditions needed for
investment on the required scale? Experience from many
other countries which run their economies on the basis of
export and investment led growth – rather than increasing
consumption – show that it certainly would. The reason why
countries as various as Switzerland, Singapore, South Korea

and China – and Germany historically – have done so well is precisely because this is the policy they have pursued. They have done it by restricting capital imports, keeping interest rates down and by having central banks intent on keeping their exchange rates competitive.

If we did engineer a truly competitive exchange rate, would the UK economy respond sufficiently strongly to make such a policy work? There is absolutely no reason to believe that this would not happen – provided that there was sufficient commitment to a sustained low parity to make investment prospects in manufacturing profitable and secure. Public sector investment depends on resources being available to pay for it, not profitability, but the reverse is true for the reindustrialisation we need. This is inevitably going to be almost entirely private-sector driven, so profitability expectations are therefore absolutely crucial.

Other objections to a competitive exchange rate strategy need to be taken seriously but are no more likely to hold us back than they do in the economies which are growing much faster than ours. A major surge in inflation is very unlikely, as is retaliation. A lower exchange rate will make us richer and not poorer.

Generally, the impact of devaluations on inflation has been low and sometimes negative – as, for example, when we came out of the ERM in 1992. Inflation also barely flickered when the pound went down in 2007/09 by 25 per cent.

As to devaluations making us poorer, of course they do in international currency – such as US dollar – terms, but UK residents do no shop in dollars but in pounds. All the evidence is that countries with more competitive currencies grow faster than those with over-valued parities – in which case GDP per head must go up and not down.

The real problem in the UK is that the exchange rate is simply ignored as a factor with a major impact on the way our economy performs. Having the right parity is just as crucial as getting monetary and fiscal policy right. It is not a silver bullet which will solve all our problems. If it is in the wrong place, however, it will undermine every other way of trying to get the UK economy to perform better.

Geoff Tily

Public spending cuts have not only damaged our public realm, they have reduced demand in the economy and so cut growth, earnings and household incomes. Higher hourly earnings and higher productivity now depend on raising demand. A new approach to public spending, including public sector wages and investment, will set the economy on a virtuous circle to faster increases in household incomes.

Since 2010, successive governments have imposed policies derived from Victorian morality rather than sound macroeconomics. Austerity coupled with attacks on workers' rights has meant a prolonged stagnation in wages and productivity, and high in-work poverty.

In this chapter I show how austerity policies have had a negative impact not only on public services, but also on economic growth, the labour market, and therefore household incomes. Boosting household incomes needs a new approach to government spending, that recognises that increasing demand will boost economic growth.

Victorian moralities

"In the end, Britain can't run away from the hard choices it faces", George Osborne.[56]

65

The goal of 'balancing the books' has been framed as a matter of morality: as well as facing up to 'hard choices', we have been told to live within our means, to take our medicine and so on.

This phoney morality has translated into actions on two main fronts. Government departments were required to cut expenditure on wages, public procurement and investment, and local authorities were hammered. Figures from the Office for Budget Responsibility (OBR) – the independent body which monitors the UK public finances – indicate that in 2022–23 public service spending per head will have been reduced by over £900 or 17 per cent.[57] At the same time, 'flexibility' was required of workers. In the face of evidence that employers were pushing workers into poor quality employment – for example through the sharp rise in zero-hours contracts – governments refused to act. They also took steps to weaken employment rights, with the introduction of employment tribunal fees, and the imposition of a Trade Union Act that sought to sharply curtail workers' rights to organise.

The blame was successfully shifted from the perpetrators of the financial crisis to the victims.

Growth failed and spending cuts continue indefinitely

All around the word cuts reduced economic growth by far more than expected by finance ministries and central banks. Figure 1 shows that in 2010, the OBR's forecast for UK GDP growth (in nominal terms) was little different from the outturn seen in the years ahead of the financial crisis. While austerity meant that the contribution of government spending to growth was cut to near zero, investment and trade were expected to compensate (columns 2 and 3). But this did not happen, and consumer demand also fell significantly short of expectations (columns 4 and 5).

Figure 1: Expenditure measure of GDP growth: annual average percentage point contributions

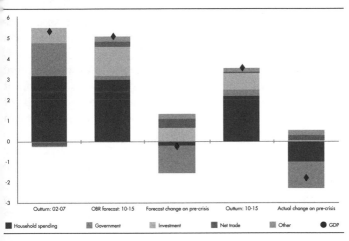

Source: ONS, OBR and TUC calculations on nominal figures

Across advanced economies, in all 32 countries where government spending growth was cut, investment and trade failed to step up to make up the shortfall. Reduced public sector spending did not 'crowd-in' the private sector, as predicted by the (not uncontentious) theories on which policymakers relied. The three countries where GDP growth went up were those where government spending growth was not cut (Germany, Israel and Japan – which will feature later).[58]

In technical terms, the evidence suggests that the multipliers that measure the impact of a change in government spending on the overall economy have been gravely underestimated. The OBR fiscal multipliers are mostly well below one (except 1.0 in the case of investment spending). This means that for every pound of government spending cut, the overall impact on the economy is expected to be less than one pound. But the evidence from the UK suggests that the actual multiplier was more like 1.5.[59] The process is hardly unfamiliar or counter-intuitive: when the government makes cuts, public sector workers have less income to spend, so private sector businesses earn less; this translates to lower incomes in the private sector, and so less spending, and so on.

This weak growth in turn meant greatly lower government receipts, for example the OBR showed a shortfall of £85bn for financial year 2015–16.[60] Fiscal policy targets have repeatedly been missed. Public sector debt was expected to peak at 70 per cent of GDP in 2013–14; the peak is now expected in the 2017–18 financial year at 86.5 per cent of GDP.

At the time of writing, there is some crowing about the UK having finally 'balanced the books', but this technicality does not mean cuts are over. Warned of five years of cuts to public services, households have now endured eight. The OBR shows at least five years more to come. As the once boss of the civil service Lord Kerslake remarked, the sum of the parts is a "quite extraordinary" policy failure.[61]

Eighty years ago John Maynard Keynes recognised that the approach to economics that the coalition government would adopt had a crude appeal, "that its teaching, translated into practice, was austere and often unpalatable, lent it virtue".[62] Inherent to his alternative macroeconomic theory was the fact that a household budget was a wholly inappropriate way to think about the government budget. Unlike the decisions of a 'virtuous' household, government actions change the course of the economy. Cutting government spending harms rather than strengthens the resolve of the private sector.

And in the real world

Pay growth has relentlessly fallen short of prices growth. In 2017 real wages fell for the seventh time in the nine years since the global financial crisis, and the OBR does not expect wages to have returned to their pre-crisis peak even by 2022–23.

While jobs have continued to expand in line with rates ahead of the financial crisis, there has been a disproportionate shift to insecure and low-quality work, and greatly increased underemployment. The wider repercussions are obvious from other measures of welfare, not least 3.7 million workers living in poverty,[63] and growing problems with indebtedness particularly among lower-paid households.[64]

Redirecting blame: the productivity fallacy

Austerity policies were controversial, but blame for the UK's continued weak levels of GDP and earnings growth is often directed elsewhere. The eurozone crisis, poorly skilled workers, hapless managers and 'zombie' companies are all in the firing line.

In economic terms, the buck is passed when discussion turns to the productivity statistics, which compare economic output with the amount of labour input (usually the number of jobs or total hours worked). In general terms productivity is presumed synonymous with 'structural' or 'supply-side' factors. Under this view, weak productivity is not the fault of demand and policy. It is easy to see why monetary and fiscal policymakers might favour arguments that rule out policy error, but it's not so easy to see why they should go uncontested.

Now plainly there is much wrong on the supply side of the economy: a financial system that fosters speculative excess rather than productive advance, an absence of industrial planning, limited regional and sectoral policies, inadequate support for upskilling and attacks on trade unions. But these defects long predate the global financial crisis and austerity. They do not explain what changed after 2008.

In the context of the weak economic growth experienced by the UK since the global financial crisis, productivity statistics show effect not cause.

From the demand point of view, as set out above, government cuts have reduced aggregate demand and overall economic growth greatly more than expected (the previous chart shows annual GDP growth slowing to 3.5 per cent after the crisis compared to 5.3 per cent ahead of the crisis). Incomes across the economy (ie the income measure of GDP) then have to adjust to this weaker growth in spending.[65] Overall, while corporate profit growth is down a little, the large part of the adjustment has been on labour income. The critical point is that within labour income the adjustment has been done through *price* (annual wage growth fell to 1.9 per cent after the crisis compared to 4.2 per cent ahead of the crisis) rather than *quantity* (annual employment growth rose to 1.2 per cent after the financial crisis compared to 0.9 per cent before the crisis).

With the total adjustment constrained by the reduced overall economic growth, lower wage growth is effectively the flipside of disproportionately high employment growth. Productivity is therefore disproportionately low, as the result of comparing weaker output growth with higher jobs growth.[66] But it is low as the *effect* of the wages adjustment, not the *cause*. The adjustment in other countries has also been skewed to wages, but not as heavily as in the UK. So the UK has done better than many other countries on jobs, but worse on wages and productivity.

Figure 2 shows the adjustment by country, comparing annual average growth ahead of the crisis (2002–2008) and after it (2010–2016), ranking the results by the change in productivity growth over the same period. For most countries the figures are negative because growth after the crisis has tended to be much lower than before.

Figure 2: Labour adjustment by country, percentage points a year

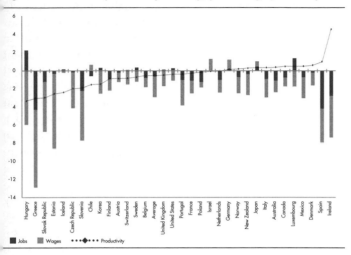

Source: OECD and TUC calculations

This is an awkward contradiction for Victorian morality, with wage flexibility and productivity opposed. But higher productivity is also a dubious virtue, brought for most countries by reduced or declined jobs growth – most obviously in Spain and Ireland.

Resolving the puzzle and undoing the errors of the past

But bringing demand into the picture shows it need not be this way. The only three countries where both wages expanded and jobs did not decline were Israel, Germany and Japan. It is not a coincidence that these are the only countries where government demand was not withdrawn.

More countries are beginning to wake up to this fact, and finally acting on the advice of the international organisations. As early as 2012 the IMF was backtracking on austerity, recognising multipliers were much higher than previously thought.[67] More recently the OECD has consistently called for higher public investment, even recognising that such spending should pay for itself.[68] Perhaps the rise of anti-establishment politics has finally incentivised politicians to pay attention.

Today's celebrated recovery elsewhere in Europe has coincided with a relatively material change of course on government spending, as well as quantitative easing on a colossal scale. For example, Ireland, Spain and Portugal have all switched from spending cuts to expansion. It is no consolation, but even in brutalised Greece government spending cuts have been greatly reduced.

This is not the case for all countries however. In many countries government spending growth has been reduced, and many countries still have very weak spending growth. The UK belongs to both categories (along with Finland, France, Japan, the Netherlands and Switzerland). Compared to major economic blocs, UK government spending is going in the wrong direction.

Table 1: Government final consumption expenditure

	Annual average growth (per cent)			Change (percentage points)	
	2002–09	2010–14	2015–17	2002–09 to 2010–14	2010–14 to 2015–17
Euro area	4.5	1.1	2.1	-3.3	0.9
United Kingdom	7.0	1.7	1.5	-5.3	-0.2
United States	5.9	1.0	2.0	-4.9	1.1
OECD	7.2	2.8	3.7	-4.4	1.0

Source: OECD Quarterly National Accounts; nominal figures to 2017Q3

Erroneous threats

The countries that have expanded fiscal policy show that self-harm can be reversed. However there are serious threats ahead as central bankers around the world are beginning to put up interest rates.

These actions are founded on the same misinterpretation. Not only have past weak outcomes been wrongly attributed to the supply-side of the economy, but the same conditions are projected into the future. The Bank of England (and the OBR) imagine a critical situation, where the degraded supply-side of the economy means that the economy cannot grow without pushing up inflation even in the face of pitifully weak demand.

The same flawed logic leads to corresponding worries about labour market conditions. With the disproportionate adjustment to wages, unemployment has fallen below rates seen ahead of the financial crisis in many countries. But the theoretical notion that low unemployment will lead to wages inflation is flatly contradicted by reality: low wages are instead leading to low unemployment, so causality is (again) the reverse of the theory. Many economists now regard this theory as bankrupt: "in addition to being morally odious, the theory is empirically unsupportable and is increasingly questioned by a younger generation of central bankers".[69]

Under these conditions the only possible justification for assuming supply as the key factor would be the actual manifestation of inflation. But inflation is dormant across all advanced economies (leaving aside the time-limited effects of the depreciation of sterling in the UK). Fundamentally this position is consistent with demand not supply weakness.

Demand and policy

Many are now calling for investment in infrastructure to strengthen both the supply and demand sides of the economy. But the implications of the demand case are more far-reaching. The attacks on public sector wages and public sector services were not only unjust, but also macroeconomically unsound.

Reversing cuts should strengthen the private economy, permit wage increases and ultimately restore family incomes (as well as boosting government revenues and so repairing the public sector finances). A more reasoned assessment of demand, and hence recognition of more spare capacity than currently understood, should also reduce the chance of interest rate rises.

No matter how vital this change of course, there are still the deep-rooted structural flaws that need to be addressed in the medium-term. But one further matter can also be addressed immediately: the Victorian approach to the labour market must end. There was mutual respect between Keynes and the leading figures of the trade union movement, and his analysis opposed the doctrine of the past 40 years: "To suppose that a flexible wage policy is a right and proper adjunct of a system which on the whole is one of *laissez-faire* is the opposite of the truth".[70]

The 150th anniversary of the first Trades Union Congress would be a fitting moment to abandon the failed doctrine of 'flexibility'. To eradicate any traces of the grotesque Trade Union Act, and instead to strengthen union recognition, worker voice and extend the role of collective bargaining Reversed austerity and strengthened real wages would double up demand and set the economy on a virtuous circle to renewed family incomes. This is the new deal that the TUC will be marching for in London on Saturday 12 May 2018.

8: TAX AND SOCIAL JUSTICE: WHY WE NEED TO REBALANCE TAXES FOR INCOMES TO GROW

Anneliese Dodds

In the last few years tax has become less fair, with the wealthiest benefiting at the expense of the majority. If typical household incomes are to rise faster – on an after-tax basis – tax increases must be targeted on those who can afford to pay. Labour will build a more progressive taxation system to fairly generate the revenues we need to ensure rising living standards and decent public services.

Most of the chapters in this pamphlet examine how to boost the pre-tax earnings of typical households. But living standards also depend on how much people pay in tax – and the quality of public services and quantity of social security they receive in return.

Over the last eight years government has chosen to cut public spending, while reducing the taxes paid by the very best-off people. It has also presided over a change in the balance of taxation, with the types of taxes paid by the wealthy being cut at the expense of those paid by everyone. Labour will take a different approach, reversing some of the reductions in taxes for the best-off, to ensure rising living standards, fair taxes and decent public services.

One of the most significant changes in modern tax systems has been a shift away from corporation taxes and towards consumption and other indirect taxes, concomitant with reductions in the top rates of income tax. This has significantly reduced the extent to which modern tax systems are progressive engines of income redistribution – as well as being sources for the funds needed to pay for public services and other public goods.

This trend has been turbo-charged in Britain. Indirect taxes such as VAT and duties now hit the poorest British peoples' disposable incomes twice as hard as the richest,[71] and the proportion of overall tax revenue coming from VAT has increased over time. This has occurred simultaneously with a big reduction in corporation tax rates. Although revenue from corporation tax increased last year, much of this was due to banks returning to profitability after the financial crisis. Between 2007–8 and 2020–21 revenues from corporation taxes as a share of overall tax revenue will have dropped by almost a third.[72] If these developments continue, the most profitable businesses and best-off people will end up paying less, while everyone else has to pick up the tab.

This chapter briefly sets out why and how we need to reset our tax system. We need to go in a different, more progressive direction, in order to support our struggling public services, redistribute income and, ultimately, ensure a fairer society where wealth is more equitably shared.

The current tax system: a block on equality and opportunity

Income tax, national insurance contributions ('NICs') and VAT make up more than half of all British taxes, while duties and other indirect taxes, and corporation taxes, amount to about a further tenth each.[73] Conservative MPs frequently maintain that because the top 1 per cent per cent currently pay a high share of income tax revenues – 28 per cent this year – this suggests the tax system is progressive.[74] In reality, given that the top income tax rate was cut, this merely reflects the recent recovery in incomes of the very best-off n Britain, and is hardly a cause for celebration. In England and Wales, Labour would of course reverse the cut in the top income tax rate, to its previous 50 per cent rate for earnings above £123,000, and would lower the threshold for the 45p additional rate to £80,000.[75]

But Labour would also focus on other areas where we see the strongest blocks to social mobility, equality and higher living standards for the many. This would start to reverse the current situation where, when all taxes are taken into account, the poorest tenth of people pay 42 per cent of their gross income in tax, compared with 34 per cent of the gross income of the top tenth of people being paid in taxes.[76]

The main rate of corporation tax will have been cut by over a third under the Tories, from 28 per cent in 2010 to 17 per cent by 2020. Indeed, Theresa May has committed herself to reducing UK corporation tax so that it is at the lowest rate out of all G20 countries. Whether May committed herself to this reduction knowing that President Trump was about to promote a 15 per cent rate is unclear. Either way, existing cuts in corporation tax in Britain have done little to induce additional investment, the justification most often rolled out by the Tories for the cut. With private sector investment in the UK still below pre-crisis levels, unlike in many comparable countries, it appears that corporation tax cuts are mainly benefiting those who receive a slice of the profits. Labour would return corporation tax rates back to 26 per cent, and reintroduce a small business rate, eventually at 21 per cent. We would also restore the banking levy to its previous level; now is not the time to be reducing the financial sector's contribution to pay for the public goods we all benefit from.

Labour would also cancel the recent reduction in inheritance tax, whereby the tax-free allowance from a couple has been increased to £1m. Only a very small proportion of

British people pay inheritance tax – just 3.9 per cent of all deaths in 2014–5 led to an inheritance tax charge, according to the most recent figures from the Office for National Statistics.[77] The recent inheritance tax cut will only serve to entrench social inequality, at a time when social mobility for the current generation of young people is 'getting worse not better' according to the government's own watchdog.[78] And Labour would not be cutting stamp duty at a time when the very tight housing market means that the government's cut will mainly help sellers not first-time buyers.

A planned approach

A key element of Labour's approach to tax is, unlike the Tories' reckless approach, to avoid nasty surprises. One of many reasons why the Conservatives' last election manifesto was so unpopular was its abandonment of the insurance principle for social care, with its new, individualised, social care property levy. Instead, Labour's Communities and Local Government team is carrying out a proper review of local taxation and local authority funding – examining the situation in different areas of the country and considering how local revenue needs can be met in a planned, predictable and equitable manner. We are also carefully considering how non-residential land value could be assessed within the tax system.

Labour's approach is of course in radical contrast to the current situation. Council tax has become increasingly regressive, especially following the devolution and reduction of funds from central government for council tax relief. This has occurred in a context where central government funding for local authorities has plummeted by around a third. The government's response to local government has been, cynically, to ask them to raise council tax[79]– yet it is those areas where people are least able to pay higher council taxes, that tend to have the biggest funding shortfalls.

More accountability, better targeting

Another area for change concerns the increasing use of taxes – and reductions in them – to achieve public policy goals. Labour can, of course, accept some of the responsibility for widening the scope of tax-related measures, given that we created the system of working and child tax credits. But these credits had a decisive, and positive, impact on family incomes – and especially on child poverty.[80] The current government is instead using tax-related measures in often regressive ways.

Support for childcare offers a clear example where the government's use of tax reliefs (the new 'tax-free childcare' system) will, if other forms of support are withdrawn, lead to a less progressive system than previously existed. The same is true of the huge rise in the income tax personal allowance seen in recent years. People on the very lowest incomes – often women – are simply unable to benefit from further increases in the income tax threshold. Indeed, when social security cuts are taken into account, the incomes of the worst-off people, especially lone parents, have decreased substantially over recent years.[81]

Instead, we need much stronger coordination between the Treasury and the Department of Work and Pensions, to consider the combined impact of tax and social security changes on peoples' incomes; as well as closer coordination between the Treasury and the Ministry for Housing, Communities and Local Government.[82]

We also need a much more transparent and open debate about tax reliefs in general. The value of tax reliefs has increased substantially in recent years, with some estimates

suggesting they amount to more than a fifth of GDP[83] – ye
there is cursory examination of them at best, certainly wher
compared to public spending of equivalent value. This is a
particular concern when many analyses of reliefs in other
countries suggest that they overwhelmingly benefit the
better-off.[84] As a result, we have committed to conduct-
ing an immediate expert review of reliefs upon entering
government.[85] Under this government the Office for Tax
Simplification has only been allowed to review tax reliefs
in a 'revenue neutral' way – i.e. only if it binds itself not to
propose reductions to the value of these reliefs. In a context
of strained government resources, that makes no sense, and
is why we are in a process of examining how reliefs can be
better accounted for and, if necessary, altered, to get the
public policy outcomes we want.

Improvements in collection

Britain's shift away from corporation taxes and towards
consumption taxes has often been linked to the ease of
collection. Indeed, some economists argue that consumption
taxes should form an even greater proportion of tax revenues, because of their ease of collection. That is to assume,
however, that tax authorities' capacities cannot be increased.
HMRC's headcount has reduced by a sixth since 2010, and
its national restructuring plan is haemorrhaging trained and
experienced staff. This is despite the fact that highly-skilled
tax experts bring in much more tax revenue than the cost of
employing them.

There is also much more that can be done to remove loop-
holes and tighten up existing measures, especially when
it comes to dealing with so-called 'profit shifting' – where
multinationals move profits between countries in order
to avoid tax. Labour's tax transparency and enforcement

programme[86] sets out a range of measures which would boost our ability to stop up holes in our leaky tax system.

Summary: how taxes can work better for families and society

Conservative tax reforms have served as a block on equality, social mobility and decent living standards. In recent years income taxes on the best-off, inheritance tax, and corporation taxes have all been cut, when the money from them could have been invested in our heavily strained public services.

Labour's planned approach would reorientate the system towards the interests of the 95 per cent, by increasing the taxes paid by those right at the top and working towards a fairer approach to local taxation and tax reliefs. The impact of these changes would be diluted, however, if current levels of tax avoidance and evasion continue. So the capacity of HMRC, both legally and in staffing terms, has to be substantially increased too. In this way we can make our tax system decisively more progressive, fairer, more transparent – and with the revenue the tax system generates, bring a boost to families' quality of life.

9: GREEN AND GROWING: HOW THE GREEN ECONOMY CAN BRING HIGHER INCOMES

Dustin Benton

The green economy is an essential ingredient in achieving higher household living standards. A strategy for clean growth and support for green industries will not only improve the environment but also increase productivity, exports and good jobs. But the UK's remarkable success in clean growth will only be maintained through long-term, cross-party consensus.

The UK's economy grew by 1.7 per cent in 2017, buoyed up by the first synchronised bout of global growth since the financial crisis. Favourable global economic conditions have raised the UK's economic output, and although the UK is the slowest growing economy in the G7, relative economic stability has blunted some of the debate over why people feel the economy is no longer working for them.[87] But the underlying concerns about why the economy hasn't raised real household incomes have not been resolved, including a persistent trade deficit, the hollowing out of the labour market, and a decade of low productivity growth.

Except there is one part of the economy that is working for people: the green economy. In 2016, the last year for which there is data, it grew at 5 per cent.[88] It has maintained similar rates of growth since the financial crisis. And it has done so while major underlying technologies have become subsidy-free: offshore wind's cost fell from around £150/MWh in 2013 to below £60/MWh in 2017. It is a vindication of a strand of the

83

UK's low carbon industrial strategy in which all three major parties had a hand: Labour's Ed Miliband and Lord Mandelson began it, Vince Cable and Ed Davey of the Liberal Democrats supported the offshore wind industry as it matured, and Conservatives Amber Rudd and Claire Perry guaranteed that the government will continue buying it through the 2020s.

Family incomes, industrial success, and economy-wide growth are not the same thing, but the former cannot grow without the latter two. And again offshore wind provides a good example of how growth and industry can underpin good quality jobs: there are around 10,000 direct jobs in offshore wind in the UK today, and this figure will likely double by 2032. The vast majority of these are skilled manual labour, technical professionals, and management jobs, which tend to support high wages, high working standards, and long tenure.[89]

More broadly, clean growth appears to be working to decouple economic growth from environmental impact. The UK's emissions – even on a consumption basis, which accounts for emissions generated overseas to make the products that the UK consumes – have fallen since 1990 while headline economic growth has risen. So long as the UK can continue this trend, it should be able to meet its 2050 carbon targets while continuing to growth in headline GDP terms.

Productivity through clean growth

Clean growth creates the conditions for good quality jobs and rising family incomes in three ways. First, the green economy can help to address the UK's persistent productivity gap. The average UK manufacturer spends five times as much on resource costs as on labour, so there is much more scope to raise productivity via resource efficiency than by cutting labour costs. For example, the best manufacturers have improved their energy efficiency by 50 per cent over en years, whilst the rest have only achieved 10–15 per cent.[90] Closing this gap would allow businesses to pay employees well while maintaining their competitiveness and cutting their environmental impact.

A focus on resource productivity would have the added benefit of reducing the UK's regional economic disparities. Those areas in the UK with a larger manufacturing economy also have lower overall productivity. A manufacturing advice service that supported resource productivity, alongside targeted innovation spending into resource efficiency technologies for manufacturers, would automatically benefit lagging areas more, helping to close the gap with London and the south-east.

Figure 1: Clean growth as a source of exports

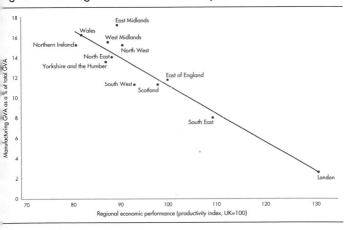

Source: Green Alliance (Lean and Clean)

Clean growth as a source of exports

The second way the green economy can support family incomes lies in the simple fact that the global economy is going green and the UK will need to grow its exports if it is to maintain growing incomes. Already, 39 per cent of the global economy is governed by states and regions that are legally committed to cutting emissions by at least 80 per cent by 2050. Investment in renewables globally was double that of fossil fuels in 2016. This is a big part of the reason that engineering giants like GE and Siemens have announced tens of thousands of job losses in their gas turbines divisions while they continue to grow their renewables businesses.[91] The lesson for workers is clear: get a green job because this is what the world is buying.

Looking only at the clean growth opportunities in emerging economies, the UK could grow its share of low carbon services by £12.5–£16bn by 2030.[92] These will be key markets for UK companies as Brexit reduces the scope for trade with the EU. Looking at goods, the story is more mixed: the chemicals industry has a £3bn trade surplus in GVA terms, above-average productivity and good quality employment, but has no plausible route to decarbonisation that doesn't include carbon capture and storage. This technology suffered a severe blow in 2016 when the UK decided not to fund a long-running CCS competition.

More positively, the UK has a £5bn trade deficit in the automotive sector but a head start in the technology that is likely to dominate the future of cars and vans: electric vehicles.[93] Nissan's Sunderland plant is the largest EV manufacturing plant in Europe. The fact that there are now substantial waiting times for buyers of electric vehicles suggests a lack of supply. Taken together, these factors – the UK's trade deficit in conventional vehicles, its head-start in EVs, and robust demand – shows that the UK should not hesitate to reorient its manufacturing base toward electric vehicles.[94] This would best be achieved by moving the UK's 2040 conventional vehicles ban forward to 2030, and by adopting a zero emissions vehicles mandate, modelled on the equivalent policies in California and China.

The alternative strategy of moving gradually would mean a decline in the automotive sector. This is especially likely if Brexit places the UK outside the single market and customs union, because of the just-in-time supply chains on which the automotive sector depends. As transport sector jobs are higher than average productivity, it's likely that replacement jobs would lower productivity, and therefore only be able to support slower wage growth.

Addressing the hollowing out of the UK's labour market

The third way that the green economy can support rising family incomes is by providing employment at intermediate skill levels that have been hit hard by the so-called hollowing out of the labour market – because mid-skill, mid-earning jobs have been at the heart of previous periods of robust family income growth. Modelling that Green Alliance undertook in 2015 showed that if the UK introduced policy akin to the EU's circular economy package, it would create around 205,000 jobs, 54,000 of which would be taken by people who were unemployed.[95] Because circular economy activity, encompassing remanufacturing, recycling, servitisation and repair, is well correlated to skill levels that have been hollowed out by mechanisation and globalisation, these jobs are likely to reduce structural, and not just cyclical, unemployment.

The story of good quality jobs that fit the UK's workforce is true at the level of individual jobs too. Green jobs, particularly those in circular economy activities, have four characteristics that make them likely to support good family incomes. First, workers in circular economy jobs are less likely to be underemployed, with fewer than 6 per cent of people in circular industries suffering inadequate hours, compared to an average of nearly 10 per cent across all other employees in the UK. Second, 40 per cent fewer people in circular economy jobs are seeking alternative employment, compared to the average worker. This suggests that they have higher job satisfaction. Third, remanufacturing jobs, which would make up the bulk of UK circular economy employment, tend to have somewhat longer tenure than the average job. And finally, 90 per cent of the jobs created through circular economy activity are likely to be around for at least a decade, despite the effects of continued digitalisation and mechanisation of employment.[96]

Figure 2: Jobs created by the circular economy could match the previous experience of the unemployed

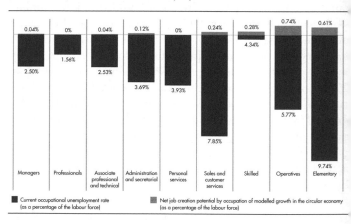

Source: Green Alliance (Employment and the Circular Economy)

What should politicians do?

The UK should move as rapidly as possible to a strategy of clean growth and a greening of the whole economy. This would of course improve the environment, but it would also underpin good family incomes.

At the level of international and particularly trade policy, the UK's best strategy is to maintain or better, to improve its high environmental standards, as these underpin its clean economy. No matter what the eventual relationship that the UK strikes with the EU, it should stay close to and seek to influence EU standards, for the simple reason that there are currently two regulatory superpowers in the world: the US and the EU. These standards are essential to clean energy, electric vehicles, green finance, and the very large UK professional services market, which had a trade surplus of £24bn in GVA terms in 2016.[97] The contrasting suggestion, made by Boris Johnson, that the UK "should be thinking not of EU standards but of global standards" ignores the fact that it is regional trade blocs that ultimate set global standards, not the other way around.[98]

At the level of industrial policy, the government has identified clean growth and future mobility as two of four of its grand challenges, noting that clean growth is "one of the *most* significant and *foreseeable* global economic trends of our time, representing one of the greatest industrial opportunities".[99] There is a disjuncture between the government's significant innovation spending and its resistance to regulate for zero carbon homes or to support heavy manufacturing in decarbonising. But the overall direction of the industrial strategy is right.

At a political level however, this industrial transition poses challenges alongside the opportunities. When Jeremy Corbyn spoke to Labour's alternative models of ownership conference in February 2018, he addressed one of the main concerns of some of his most stalwart supporters: that the energy transition will put them out of work. As he put it: "Many people and communities in Britain are economically reliant on fossil fuels."[100]

The fossil fuel industry has provided good quality, well-paid, high-skill jobs – often unionised – which have lasted for decades. As these jobs decline due both to the pollution they cause and competition from clean energy and transport, a leader with Corbyn's concerns is right to outline a 'just transition', that recreates the character, quality, and longevity of the jobs that are being replaced. The evidence that Green Alliance has marshalled shows that it is possible to clean up while keeping quality jobs.

Corbyn's promise is that: "In public hands, under democratic control, workforces and their unions will be the managers of this change, not its casualties." But his shorter formulation was "to go green, we must take control of our energy".

This is a much stronger claim. In fact, the UK's experience of halving power sector emissions since 2012 shows that it is possible to go green without public ownership.[101] Of course politicians should fight over how *best* to address climate change, and nationalisation is popular: 77 per cent of voters support it.[102] But politicians should not fall into the trap of stating that the pressing issue of climate change has only one solution. The UK's remarkable success in clean growth is built upon a deliberately non-partisan Climate Act that emphasises multiple routes to a low carbon future. The contrast of the United States, in which tribal politics has prevented Republicans from supporting clean growth and thereby undermined Democratic efforts to generate it, is a salutary warning.

A green economy will create good quality growth. Governed well, it can raise family incomes and support a fairer society. But it can only do if it maintains the wide consensus that has allowed it to grow through administrations led by Labour, Lib Dem, and Conservative ministers.

ENDNOTES

1   Rachel Reeves, 'Labour's Class Coalitions: Then and Now', Political Quarterly, (Vol.88, No.4, 2017), 702-6.

2   Cameron Tait, A Good Day's Work: What workers think about work, and how politics should respond, (London: Fabian Society, 2016).

3   Colin Crouch, 'Privatised Keynesianism: An Unacknowledged Policy Regime', British Journal of Politics and International Relations, (Vol. 11, No.3, 2009), pp.382–399.

4   Cameron Tait, Productivity and Pay: The Fabian Society's Retail Industry Task Force, (London: Fabian Society, 2017).

5   Nita Clarke, 'People are the solution to the productivity puzzle', in Yvette Cooper MP (ed.), Changing Work: Progressive Ideas for the Modern World of Work, (London: Fabian Society, 2016), pp.41–8.

6   Stuart MacDonald, 'Industrial Strategy: Foundations in the Right Place?', Centre for Local Economic Strategies, cles.org.uk/blog/industrial-strategy-foundations-in-the-right-place/

7   Gavin Kelly and Dan Tomlinson, 'The Future of Trade Unionism and the Next Generation', in Nick Tyrone (ed.), The Future of Trade Unionism in Britain, (Radix, 2016), pp.10-15; see also, Cameron Tait and Tobias Phibbs (eds), A New Collectivism: How private sector trade unions can innovate and grow, (London: Fabian Society, 2018).

8   Tom Hunt and Sean McDaniel, 'Tackling insecure work: Political actions from around the world', SPERI, speri.dept.shef.ac.uk/wp-content/uploads/2017/09/Tackling-insecure-work-political-actions-from-around-the-world-SPERI-report-for-GMB.pdf

9   John McDonnell MP, speech to Alternative Models of Ownership conference, 10th February 2018.

10 www.resolutionfoundation.org/app/uploads/2018/02/IC-labour-market-policy.pdf

11 Defined as mean disposable household income after taxes and benefits have been accounted for.

12 Office for National Statistics (ONS) (2018) Household disposable income and inequality in the UK: financial year ending 2017. Statistical Bulletin.

13 Defined as people with disposable income below 60% of the median.

14   Atkinson, Antony, Hasell, Joe, Morelli, Salvatore, and Roser, Max (2017) The Chartbook of Economic Inequality. The Institute for New Economic Thinking at the Oxford Martin School.

15   AMECO – Annual macro-economic database by the European Commission. Online: ec.europa.eu/economy_finance/ameco/user/serie/SelectSerie.cfm [Accessed: January 2018].

16   Guschanski, Alexander and Onaran, Özlem (2017) The political economy of income distribution: industry level evidence from 14 OECD countries. Greenwich Papers in Political Economy, University of Greenwich Business School, London.

17   Guschanski, Alexander and Onaran, Özlem (2018) The labour share and financialisation: Evidence from publicly listed firms. Greenwich Papers in Political Economy, Business School, London.

18   Onaran, Özlem and Obst, Thomas (2016) Wage-led growth in the EU15 member states: the effects of income distribution on growth, investment, trade balance, and inflation. Cambridge Journal of Economics, 40(6):1517–1551. Onaran, Özlem and Galanis, Giorgos (2014) Income distribution and growth: a global model. Environment and Planning A, 46:2489–2513. Stockhammer, Engelbert and Onaran, Özlem (2004). Accumulation, distribution and employment: a structural VAR approach to a Kaleckian macro model. Structural Change and Economic Dynamics, 15(4):421–447.

19   Onaran, Özlem and Obst, Thomas (2016 Wage-led growth in the EU15 member states: the effects of income distribution on growth, investment, trade balance, and inflation. Cambridge Journal of Economics, 40(6):1517–1551.

20   IMF (2009), Global Economic Policies and Prospects, Note by the Staff of the International Monetary Fund, G20 Meeting of the Ministers and Central Bank Governors, March 13–14, 2009, London. Dabla-Norris, Era Kochhar, Kalpana, Suphaphiphat, Nujin Ricka, Frantisek, and Tsounta, Evridiki (2015) Causes and Consequences of Income Inequality: A Global Perspective. IMF Staff Discussion Note 15/13, International Monetary Fund, Washington. Ostry, Jonathan, Berg, Andrew and Tsangarides, Charalambos (2014) "Redistribution, Inequality, and Growth". IMF Staff Discussion Note 14/02, International Monetary Fund, Washington. Foerster, M. and Cingano, F. 2014. Trends in Income Inequality and its Impact on Economic Growth. Paris: OECD.

21   Obst, Thomas, Onaran, Özlem and Nikolaidi, Maria (2017) The effect of income distribution and fiscal policy on growth, investment, and budget balance: the case of Europe. Greenwich Papers in Political Economy, University of Greenwich Business School, London.

22   Onaran, Özlem and Obst, Thomas (2016) Wage-led growth in the EU15 member states: the effects of income distribution on growth, investment, trade balance, and inflation. Cambridge Journal of Economics, 40(6):1517–1551. Obst, Thomas, Onaran, Özlem and Nikolaidi, Maria (2017) The effect of income distribution and fiscal policy on growth, investment, and budget balance: the case of Europe. Greenwich Papers in Political Economy, University of Greenwich Business School, London.

23 Comparison between the value of ONS code YBEZ for 2017 Q3 and 2007 Q3. London ONS, December 2017.

24 This is an extrapolation of the increase in the UK population between 2006 and 2016, the latest years for which exact figures are available. Page 829 in International Financial Statistics Yearbook 2017. Washington DC: IMF 2017.

25 ONS Time Series code NPQT divided by YBHA.

26 Estimates produced by numerous organisations, including the Bank of England, the IMF, OECD and the Office for Budget Responsibility.

27 Page 86 in International Financial Statistics Yearbook 2017. Washington DC: IMF, 2017.

28 ONS Time Series code NPQT divided by YHBA.

29 ONS codes NPQT minus EQDO divided by YBHA. London, ONS, December 2017.

30 ONS code DLWO – "Other machinery and equipment" is used as the best available proxy.

31 Consumption of Fixed Capital in the UK was 12.9% of GDP in 2016. Page 829 in International Financial Statistics Yearbook 2017. Washington DC: IMF 2017.

32 Economics Help website.

33 Calculations based on ONS codes ABMI and YBEX. London: ONS, December 2017.

34 Data from Trading Economics website. At the end of 2017 wages in manufacturing averaged £595 per week compared to an overall average of £510.

35 ONS Times Series codes BOKI compared to IKBD.

36 ONS Time Series for code IKBJ published in December 2017.

37 ONS codes IKBG divided by YBHA. London: ONS December 2017.

38 ONS Time Series codes ELBH plus ELBI. London, ONS, December 2017.

39 ONS Time Series code IKBJ. London: ONS, December 2017.

40 ONS Data Series code IKBD. London: ONS, December 2017.

41 ONS Time Series code BOKI. London: ONS, December 2017.

42 ONS Time Series code HBOP. London, ONS, December 2017.

43 ONS Time Series code HBOP. London, ONS, December 2017.

44 ONS Time Series code HBOP. London, ONS, December 2017.

45 ONS Time Series for IKBP/ London: ONS, December 2017.

46 Page 32 in the 2010 International Financial Statistics Yearbook, and page 33 in the 2017 edition. Washington DC: IMF.

47 Economics Help website.

48 Table 1.1. in GVA by Region. London: ONS, 2014.

49 Page 7 in Economic Review, March 2014. London: ONS, 2014.

50 www.theguardian.com/news/datablog/2011/jan/interest-rates-since-1694.

51 The abolition of the Monopolies and Merger Commission in 1999 and its replacement by the Competition Commission, and the 2002 Enterprise Act.

52 Table 7.1, page 66, in the 2011 the ONS Pink Book. London: ONS, 2011.

53 ONS Time Series code YBHA. London: ONS, December 2017.

54 Page 745 in International Financial Statistics Yearbook 2010. Washington DC: IMF 2010.

55   See Call to Action by John Mills and Bryan Gould. London: Ebury Publishing, 2015.

56   George Osborne, Daily Telegraph, 28 January 2013. www.telegraph.co.uk/news/politics/9831687/George-Osborne-We-cannot-run-from-hard-choices-on-the-economy.html

57   'Budget was all talk and not action', Kate Bell, TUC blog, 22 November 2017, www.tuc.org.uk/blogs/budget-2017-was-all-talk-and-no-action

58   'Note to Philip Hammond: In ALL 32 OECD countries that cut spending, economic growth was seriously damaged', Geoff Tily, Touchstone blog, 14 July 2016, touchstoneblog.org.uk/2016/07/phillip-hammond-32-32-oecd-countries-spending-cut-economic-growth-significantly-damaged/

59   Why Multipliers Matter, Geoff Tily, Touchstone blog, 24 July 2017, touchstoneblog.org.uk/2017/07/why-multipliers-matter/

60   Office for Budget Responsibility, Forecast evaluation report, October 2016, Chart 1.1, page 5.

61   'Kerslake review of Treasury warns that austerity has failed', Geoff Tily, Touchstone blog, 13 February 2017, touchstoneblog.org.uk/2017/02/kerslake-review-treasury-warns-austerity-failed/

62   John Maynard Keynes (1936) The General Theory of Employment Interest and Money, p. 33.

63   UK Poverty 2017, Joseph Roundtree Foundation, December 2017, www.jrf.org.uk/report/uk-poverty-2017

64   The case for a household debt Jubilee', Jubilee Debt Campaign and The Centre for Responsible Credit, 6 March 2018, jubileedebt.org.uk/press-release/campaigners-call-for-household-debt-jubilee-to-address-billions-of-unjust-debt]

65   The process is set out in more detail in 'Productivity: no puzzle about it', Trades Union Congress, February 2015, www.tuc.org.uk/sites/default/files/productivitypuzzle.pdf

66   See also: 'The Productivity Fallacy', Geoff Tily, Royal Economics Society Newsletter, July 2016: www.res.org.uk/view/art5aJul16Features.html

67   In their October 2012 World Economic Outlook, the IMF admitted: "Our results indicate that multipliers have actually been in the 0.9 to 1.7 range since the Great Recession".

68   'Using the fiscal levers to escape the low-growth trap', OECD, November 2016. They observe: "To the extent that monetary policy is constrained, an investment-led stimulus may raise output more than it increases debt, leading to a fall in the debt-to-GDP ratio in the short term. This will likely be the case if public investment manages to catalyse private investment". www.oecd.org/eco/using-fiscal-levers-to-escape-the-low-growth-trap.htm

69   'NAIRU: not just bad economics, now also bad politics', Matthew Klein, Financial Times Alphaville, 24 January 2018. ftalphaville.ft.com/2018/01/24/2198028/nairu-not-just-bad-economics-now-also-bad-politics/

70   Keynes (ibid.) p. 269.

71   www.ons.gov.uk/peoplepopulationandcommunity/personalandhousehold-
      finances/incomeandwealth/bulletins/theeffectsoftaxesandbenefitsonhouse-
      holdincome/financialyearending2016#main-points

72   www.ifs.org.uk/uploads/publications/bns/BN_182.pdf, p.5.

73   www.ifs.org.uk/uploads/publications/bns/bn09.pdf, p.4.

74   www.hansard.parliament.uk/commons/2017-11-01/debates/4ECBE712-
      2E2C-44B5-9B9B-72B1A816D078/Engagements#Column813

75   Income tax is a devolved matter, so Scottish income tax rates are set by the
      Scottish government.

76   www.ons.gov.uk/peoplepopulationandcommunity/personalandhousehold-
      finances/incomeandwealth/datasets/theeffectsoftaxesandbenefitsonhouse-
      holdincomefinancialyearending2014

77   www.gov.uk/government/uploads/system/uploads/attachment_data/
      file/632797/IHTNationalStatisticsCommentary.pdf

78   www.gov.uk/government/uploads/system/uploads/attachment_data/
      file/662744/State_of_the_Nation_2017_-_Social_Mobility_in_Great_Britain.
      pdf, p.iii.

79   www.hansard.parliament.uk/commons/2018-02-27/debates/b1639714-46fa-
      45ff-88f9-a7dab5e11711/CommonsChamber

80   www.resolutionfoundation.org/app/uploads/2014/08/Creditworthy.pdf

81   www.cpag.org.uk/sites/default/files/Austerity per cent20Generation per
      cent20FINAL.pdf

82   lfig.org/publications/the-kerslake-review-of-the-treasury/

83   www.nao.org.uk/wp-content/uploads/2014/03/Tax-reliefs.pdf, p.8.

84   Faricy, C., 2016, Welfare for the wealthy: parties, social spending and inequal-
      ity in the US, Cambridge: Cambridge University Press.

85   labour.org.uk/wp-content/uploads/2017/10/Funding-Britains-Future.pdf

86   labour.org.uk/wp-content/uploads/2017/10/Tax-transparency-
      programme.pdf

87   uk.reuters.com/article/uk-britain-economy/graphic-brexit-vote-impact-felt-
      throughout-uk-economy-idUKKCN1GB1C2

88   www.ons.gov.uk/economy/environmentalaccounts/bulletins/finalesti-
      mates/2016

89   aurawindenergy.com/uploads/files/Cambride-Econometrics-Future-UK-
      Employment-in-Offshore-Wind-June-2017.pdf

90   www.green-alliance.org.uk/resources/Lean_and_clean.pdf

91   See www.reuters.com/article/us-siemens-power-restructuring/siemens-
      says-to-cut-about-6900-jobs-idUSKBN1DG257 and www.bloomberg.com/
      news/articles/2017-12-07/ge-is-said-to-plan-12-000-job-cuts-as-new-ceo-
      revamps-power-unit

92   greenallianceblog.org.uk/2017/04/21/how-uk-plc-can-support-emerging-
      economies-to-go-low-carbon/

93   www.green-alliance.org.uk/resources/UK_trade_in_a_decarbonising_
      world.pdf

94   www.electrive.com/2018/02/19/electric-cars-got-delivery-problem-
      across-board/

95   www.green-alliance.org.uk/employment-and-the-circular-economy.php
96   www.green-alliance.org.uk/resources/Job%20quality%20in%20a%20circular%20economy.pdf
97   www.green-alliance.org.uk/resources/Lean_and_clean.pdf
98   www.gov.uk/government/speeches/foreign-secretary-speech-uniting-for-a-great-brexit
99   www.gov.uk/government/uploads/system/uploads/attachment_data/file/672137/Government_Response_to_unabated_coal_consultation_and_statement_of_policy.pdf
100 labour.org.uk/press/jeremy-corbyn-speech-alternative-models-ownership-conference/
101 www.bbc.co.uk/news/uk-42495883
102 www.theguardian.com/business/2017/oct/01/jeremy-corbyn-nationalisation-plans-voters-tired-free-markets

JOIN THE FABIANS TODAY
Join us and receive at least four pamphlets or books a year as well as our quarterly magazine, Fabian Review.

I'd like to become a Fabian

Standard Rate: £4 per month
Concessions (under-21s, student, unwaged or retired): £2 per month

Name	Date of birth
Address	Postcode
Email	
Telephone	

Instruction to Bank   Originator's ID: 971666

Bank/building society name	
Address	**DIRECT Debit**
Acct holder(s)	Postcode
Acct no.	Sort code

I instruct you to pay direct debits from my account at the request of the Fabian Society. The instruction is subject to the safeguards of the Direct Debit Guarantee.

Signature	Date

Return to:
Fabian Society Membership
FREEPOST RTEG – XLTU – AEJX
61 Petty France, London SW1H 9EU